BAKING *With My* ANKARSRUM

STAND MIXER

Easy To Follow Recipes By *Kerry Megaw*

TABLE OF CONTENTS

COOKIES

SLICES AND BARS

CAKE

DESSERT

LOAF

OTHER

BREAD

This book is dedicated to Colin, Jackson, Flynn, and my little companions Doc and Luna.

A BIT ABOUT ME..

Hi, I'm Kerry. I have called Christchurch, New Zealand home my whole life, apart from 14 years living in Perth and Sydney, Australia. I have always loved cooking, especially baking, and when my sons were young I enjoyed sending them off to school with a plate of something to share.

As my son Flynn started travelling to competitions with his school Jazz Band, I became their resident cook and baker and earned the nickname "Kerry Slice" from all the home baking I would bring along that would quickly disappear.

I'd always dreamt about opening my own little café, and when my sons left school I got to accomplish my dream by opening Wycola Kitchen. It was small enough that I could do all the baking myself from scratch, and so I got to spend all day doing what I loved.

While running my café, I also undertook an apprenticeship as a pastry baker and graduated at the grand old age of 55. I later sold my café, however I still love making pastry in my she-shed and sharing the results with friends and family.

Like many others, I loved the idea of the Ankarsrum for making pastry. However, I initially struggled with it and was left disappointed with the limited selection of recipes available. I grew to love it, and I loved experimenting with what it could do. It seemed like there were many others online who were struggling with the same problems, and so I decided to roll up my sleeves and write my favourite recipes for the "Ank" for others to enjoy so they could love it and make the most of it as well.

As well as baking I love photography, and so all the photos in this book were taken by me on my kitchen table. There are no hidden tricks, if you follow the instructions, you'll get the same results as seen in the photos.

I hope you enjoy this recipe book as much as I enjoyed writing it!

INGREDIENTS

Superfine Sugar: Is also called Caster Sugar. It is slightly finer than granulated sugar, but not powdery like Confectioners' sugar. Just substitute for granulated sugar if you need to, or you could blitz granulated sugar for a few seconds in a food processor. The only recipe that it may alter is the meringues – it will take a little longer to dissolve the sugar into the egg white.

Confectioners' Sugar: Is also called Icing Sugar.

Cocoa: The weight may fluctuate depending on what brand you use. If you find the recipe a little dry, go easy on the cocoa next time. If you can, use Dutch cocoa. It's darker and richer.

Chocolate: Even if it says dark chocolate, use any chocolate you like!

Kosher Salt: or table salt.

Eggs: Medium size eggs have been used in this book – approx 50 grams each.

Cream: This is a tricky one …there are so many types, and different in every country. Just use the type of cream like you would use to whip and put on a cake, or dessert.

Golden Syrup: Can be replaced with Corn Syrup.

Mixed Spice: This is made up of cinnamon, coriander seed, cloves, ginger and nutmeg. It can be substituted for Pumpkin Pie Spice.

SHORTBREAD

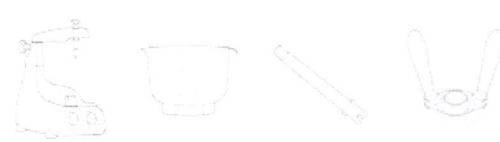

INGREDIENTS

300 grams soft butter (1 ⅓ cups)
165 grams Superfine sugar (¾ cup)
310 grams bread flour (2 ½ cups)
64 grams cornstarch (½ cup)

METHOD

1. Line 2 baking sheets with parchment paper.
2. Assemble the Ankarsrum with the beater bowl and single wire cookie whisk.
3. Place butter in the plastic beater bowl and beat at speed 3 for 1 to 2 minutes until pale and creamy.
4. Scrape down the bowl with a rubber spatula then add the sugar and beat for further 2 minutes on speed 3
5. Reduce speed to low and add flour and cornstarch then increase to speed 6 and mix for a further 1 minute until just combined. It will look like large breadcrumbs. *Don't mix it into a ball because it causes too much strain on the plastic beater gears.*
6. Squish the mixture together with your hand while in the bowl and tip out onto a lightly floured bench.
7. Either roll it into a log and wrap it in cling wrap or form it into a disk if you want to use a cookie cutter.
8. Chill in the fridge for 30 minutes.
9. Preheat oven to 230°F (110°C)
10. If you rolled the mixture into a log, slice around ½ inch (12mm) thick, and if you formed a disk, roll it out on a floured bench, cut it with cookie cutters, and place it on the prepared tray.
11. Bake for 1 hour. It should be still pale.
If you double the recipe, you must use the stainless steel bowl and roller.

TIP: When you assemble the stainless steel bowl.Move the arm to the desired position finger tighten the knob, but don't oven tighten. The arm should be able to move freely towards the middle of the bowl, but not towards the edge of the bowl.

CHOCOLATE CHUNK COOKIES

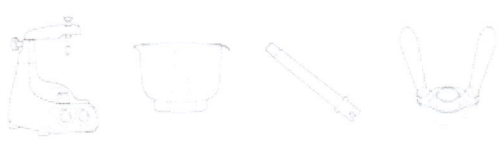

INGREDIENTS

226 grams soft butter (1 cup)
100 grams granulated sugar (½ cup)
60 grams sweetened condensed milk (¼ cup plus 1 tablespoon)
4 grams vanilla extract (1 teaspoon)
310 grams all-purpose flour (2 ½ cups)
10 grams baking powder (2 teaspoons)
240 grams chocolate; roughly chopped (1 ½ cups) white, dark or milk or mixed
55 grams pecans (½ cup)

METHOD

1. Line 2 baking sheets with parchment paper.
2. Assemble the Ankarsrum with the beater bowl and single wire cookie whisks.
3. Place butter and sugar in the Ankarsrum stainless steel bowl, and beat at speed 3 for 2 minutes, until pale and creamy.
4. Add condensed milk and vanilla and continue beating for 1 minute.
5. Scrape down the sides and add flour and baking powder. Start mixing at low, then increase speed up to speed 6 and mix for a further 1 minute or until just combined. Remove from the machine and stir in chocolate chunks and nuts. DON'T mix the chocolate or nuts with the whisks.It will damage the gears.
6. Chill for 15 minutes until the mixture is firm enough to shape and roll.
7. Preheat oven to 320°F (160°C).
8. Roll tablespoons of the mixture into balls and place on prepared trays, allowing room in between for spreading. Flatten with the palm of your hand to slightly flatten. Bake until lightly golden (about 15 minutes). Leave on the tray for 1-2 minutes, then transfer to a wire rack to cool.

TIP: If you double the recipe you must use the stainless steel bowl and roller.

SANTE COOKIES

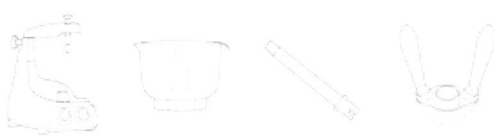

INGREDIENTS

130 grams butter, soft (½ cup plus 1 tablespoon)
50 grams granulated sugar (¼ cup)
60 grams sweetened condensed milk (¼ cup)
4 grams vanilla extract (1 teaspoon)
185 grams all-purpose flour (1½ cups)
5 grams baking powder (1 teaspoon)
85g chocolate chips (½ cup)

METHOD

1. Preheat oven to 350°F (180°C).
2. Line 2 baking sheets with parchment paper.
3. Assemble the Ankarsrum with the plastic beater bowl and single wire cookie whisk.
4. Place butter and sugar in the plastic beater bowl and beat at low speed 3 for 2 minutes, until pale and creamy.
5. Scrape down the bowl with a rubber spatula, then add condensed milk and vanilla and continue beating on 3 for 1 minute.
6. Reduce speed to low, add flour and baking powder, and continue to mix until it looks like large breadcrumbs. If it seems dry and crumbly you may need to scrape the bottom of the bowl again. Lastly, add the chocolate chips and mix until just combined, no more than 30 seconds. You don't want to over-mix because it causes strain on the plastic gears.
7. Roll tablespoons of the mixture into balls about the size of a golf ball, place on prepared trays and flatten with a floured fork.
8. Bake for 18-20 minutes until golden. Leave on the tray for 1-2 minutes then place on a wire rack to cool.

TIP: Use the roller if you double the recipe.

BELGIUM COOKIES

INGREDIENTS

130 grams soft butter, (½ cup plus 1 tablespoon)
100 grams granulated sugar (½ cup)
1 egg
250 grams all-purpose flour (2 cups)
5 grams Baking Powder (1 teaspoon)
2 grams ground cinnamon (1 teaspoon)
2 grams ground nutmeg (1 teaspoon)
2 grams ground ginger (1 teaspoon)
2 grams mixed spice (1 teaspoon)
Raspberry jam
Red Jelly crystals
Icing
180 grams confectioners' sugar (1 ½ cups)
15 grams soft butter, (1 tablespoon)
30 grams water (2 tablespoons)

METHOD

1. Assemble the Ankarsrum with the plastic beater bowl and single wire cookie whisk.

2. Line 2 baking sheets with parchment paper.

3. Place butter and sugar in the plastic beater bowl and beat at speed 3 for 2 minutes until pale and creamy. Add egg and continue to beat for 1 more minute.

4. Reduce speed to low and add flour, baking powder, cinnamon, nutmeg, ginger, and mixed spice, and then increase to speed 2 for 1- 2 minutes or until it looks like large crumbs. If it is looking dry and not coming together in big crumbs you may need to scrape the side and bottom of the bowl.

5. While it is in the bowl either squish the mixture together with your hands or tip it onto the bench and bring it together into a ball, then shape the dough into a disk and wrap it in cling wrap. Place it in the fridge for 20 minutes.

6. Preheat oven to 320°F (160°C).

7. Place dough on a floured bench or between 2 layers of parchment paper and roll out thinly. (5mm or 1/5inch) Press out with a round cookie cutter to the size you require.

8. Place on baking trays and bake for 15 minutes. Cool for 10 minutes.

9. Make Icing, by combining confectioners' sugar, and butter in a small bowl. Add just enough water to make the icing spreadable

10. Ice half of the cookies with icing and sprinkle jelly crystals on the icing while still wet, then turn over the other half of the cookies and place a dob of jam on the cookies. Then, place the iced cookies on the jam cookies and press slightly to sandwich them together.

TIP: If the dough becomes too soft when rolling it, just place it back into the fridge to firm up.

PECAN AND POPCORN COOKIES

INGREDIENTS

110 grams firmly packed brown sugar (½ cup)
100 grams granulated sugar (½ cup)
112 grams soft butter (½ cup)
4 grams vanilla extract (1 teaspoon)
1 egg
125 grams all-purpose flour (1 cup)
2.5 grams baking powder (½ teaspoon)
25g coconut (1/4 cup)
6 grams sea salt (1 teaspoon)
2 cups caramel popcorn
115 grams pecan chopped (1 cup)

METHOD

1. Preheat oven to 320°F (160°C)
2. Line 2 baking sheets with parchment paper
3. Assemble the Ankarsrum with the stainless steel bowl, scraper, and dough roller, with the roller against the edge.
4. Place both the sugars, butter, and vanilla in the Ankarsrum stainless steel bowl and beat for 2 minutes at speed 3 until pale and creamy.   If large clumps of butter and sugar are getting stuck on your scraper or roller, remove the scraper and beat on high for 2 or 3 minutes until the butter and sugar are starting to become creamed.Then place the scraper back onto the bowl to continue. It will come together when the rest of the ingredients are added.
5. Add the egg and continue for 3 minutes beating until well combined. Reduce to low, and add the flour, baking powder, coconut, and salt and increase to speed 2 beat for 1 minute or until just combined. Finally, add the popcorn and pecans and mix until just combined.
6. If some of the ingredients are not moving from the middle of the bowl slowly swing the dough roller into the middle for a few seconds to incorporate ingredients.
7. Place heaped tablespoons of the dough on prepared baking sheets, flatten slightly with the palm of your hand, and allow room to spread.
8. Bake for 15–18 minutes or until the cookies are golden. Allow to cool on a rack.

TIP: Make sure your popcorn is fully popped so there are no nasty surprises or visits to the dentist!

MELTING MOMENTS

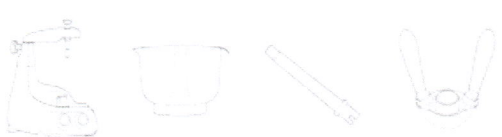

INGREDIENTS

130 grams butter, soft (1/2 cup plus 1 tablespoon)
114 grams all-purpose flour (3/4 cup plus 2 tablespoons)
40 grams confectioners' sugar sifted (1/3 cup)
24 grams cornstarch (3 tablespoons)
24 grams custard powder (3 tablespoons)
2 grams finely grated lemon zest (1 teaspoon)
15 grams lemon juice (1 tablespoon)

Icing
40 grams butter, room temperature (3 tablespoons) extra
120 grams confectioners' sugar (1 cup) extra
2 grams finely grated lemon zest, (1 teaspoon) extra
1 Tablespoon of Coloring and flavoring of your choice.
raspberry jam (optional)

METHOD

1. Preheat oven to 320°F (160°C).
2. Line 2 baking sheets with parchment paper.
3. Assemble the Ankarsrum with the beater bowl and single wire cookie whisk.
4. Place butter in the plastic beater bowl and mix on speed 3 for 2 minutes until pale and creamy. Reduce speed to low and add the flour, confectioners' sugar, cornstarch, custard powder, lemon zest, and juice and beat for a further minute until just mixed. You may need to stop and scrape the bottom of the bowl once if the butter is not quite mixed. You don't want the mixture to work itself into a ball because it causes strain on the beater gears.
5. Use your hands to roll teaspoonfuls of the dough mixture into small balls about the size of walnuts. They can be quite small because each serving is two cookies! Place the balls approx. 1 inch (3cm) apart on the lined trays. Use a fork dusted in icing sugar to flatten gently.
6. Bake for 15 minutes until just cooked through, but still pale. Remove from oven and set aside for 30 minutes to cool.

Icing
1. Assemble the Ankarsrum with the plastic beater bowl and single wire cookie whisk.
2. Add the extra butter and confectioners' sugar to the bowl and beat for 2 minutes on 3 until light and fluffy. Add lemon zest, coloring and flavoring and continue for 1 more minute.
3. Spread or pipe the butter mixture over the flat side of half the biscuits and spread jam (if using) on the other side. Then sandwich together.

AFGHAN COOKIES

  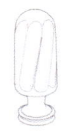 

INGREDIENTS

226 grams soft butter (1 cup)
100 grams granulated sugar (½ cup)
185 grams all-purpose flour (1 ½ cups)
44 grams cocoa (½ cup)
80 grams cornflakes (2 cups) (or Weetabix)
Walnuts pieces
Chocolate Icing
180 grams confectioners' sugar (1 ½ cups)
14 grams soft butter (1 tablespoon)
15 grams water (1 tablespoon) approx.
15 grams cocoa powder (3 tablespoons)

METHOD

1. Preheat oven to 350°F (180°C).
2. Line 2 baking sheets with parchment paper.
3. Assemble the Ankarsrum with the stainless steel bowl, dough knife, and dough roller.
4. Place butter and sugar in the Ankarsrum stainless steel bowl and beat at speed 3 for 2 minutes. If large clumps of butter and sugar are getting stuck on your scraper or roller, remove the scraper and beat on high for 2 or 3 minutes until the butter and sugar are starting to become creamed. Then, place the scraper back onto the bowl to continue. It will come together when the rest of the ingredients are added.
5. Reduce to low, add the flour and cocoa powder, gradually increasing again to speed 3 for 1 more minute.
6. Reduce speed again to low and add cornflakes until just mixed. You want them to be crunchy. If some of the ingredients are not moving in the middle of the bowl slowly move the dough roller into the middle for a few seconds to incorporate ingredients.
7. Spoon tablespoons of mixture onto the tray, gently pressing with the palm of your hand to make them slightly flat.
8. Bake for 15 minutes or until firm to touch. Leave on tray for a few minutes then transfer to a wire rack to cool completely.
9. When cold, ice with chocolate icing and decorate with a walnut piece.

Chocolate Icing:
Place confectioners' sugar, cocoa, and butter in a small bowl. Add just enough water to make the icing spreadable.

TIP: In this book, it states soft butter, rather than room temperature because how warm is your room? We have noticed that 70-degree (21-degree) butter is harder to mix (and more frustrating) than 77-degree (25-degree) butter! If your butter feels on the hard side, just weigh it, dice it into large chunks, and place it in a small bowl. Place a cup of water in the microwave and boil the water for 2 minutes, then place the butter into the microwave with the water and let it sit there for a few minutes. It will soften your butter but not melt it.

GINGERBREAD COOKIES

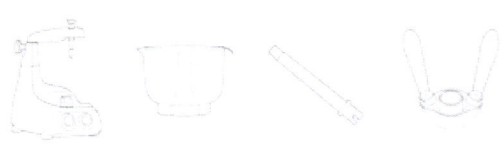

INGREDIENTS

130 grams soft butter, (1/2 cup plus 1 tablespoon)
75 grams firmly packed brown sugar (1/ 3 cup)
225 grams golden syrup/light treacle (2/3 cup)
375 grams All-purpose flour (3 cups)
5 grams baking soda (1 teaspoon)
4 grams ground ginger (2 teaspoons)
2 grams mixed spice/pumpkin pie spice (1 teaspoon)

METHOD

1. Assemble the Ankarsrum with the plastic beater bowl and single wire cookie whisk
2. Place butter and sugar in the plastic beater bowl and beat at speed 6 for 4–5 minutes until pale and creamy
3. Scrape down the sides of the bowl, and add the golden syrup, flour, bicarbonate of soda, ginger, and mixed spice. Beat at speed 3 until a smooth dough forms.
4. Roll dough out between 2 sheets of non-stick baking paper to approx. (1/8th inch) 5mm thick. Refrigerate for 30 minutes or until firm.
5. Preheat oven to 285°F (140°C).
6. Line 2 baking sheets with parchment paper.
7. Cut cookies to your desired shape.
Bake for 23–25 minutes or until golden and dry to touch. Allow to cool completely on the trays.

TIP: When you are measuring syrup or honey, drizzle a little bit of oil in the spoon or cup. It helps the syrup slip out, rather than stick.

COOKIES AND CREAM COOKIES

INGREDIENTS

226 grams butter, melted and cooled (1 cup)
165 grams superfine sugar (3/4 cup)
170 grams bittersweet chocolate, (1cup), melted and slightly cooled
1 egg, lightly beaten
220 grams all-purpose (1 ¾ cups)
44 grams cocoa (1/2 cup)
3 grams kosher salt (1 teaspoon)
2.5 grams baking soda (1/2 teaspoon)
Vanilla Cream Filling
113 grams butter, room temperature(1/2 cup)
240 grams confectioners' sugar (2 cups)
4 grams vanilla extract (1 teaspoon)
15 grams whole milk (1 Tablespoon)
Pinch of salt

METHOD

1. Line 2 baking sheets with parchment paper.
2. Assemble the Ankarsrum with the stainless steel bowl, scraper and the dough roller, with the roller against the edge.
3. Place butter and sugar in the Ankarstrum stainless steel bowl, and beat on speed 6 for 3 minutes, (If large clumps of butter and sugar are getting stuck on your scraper or roller, remove the scraper and beat on high for 2 or 3 minutes until the butter and sugar is starting to become creamed. Then place the scraper back on to bowl to continue. It will come together when the rest of the ingredients are added.)
4. Reduce the speed to 3 and add the chocolate and egg and beat for a further minute until completed incorporated.
5. Reduce the speed to low and add the flour, cocoa, salt, and baking soda in the bowl and increase speed to 2 for less than a minute until just combined. If some of the ingredients are not moving from the middle of the bowl slowly swing the dough roller into the middle for a few seconds to incorporate ingredients.
6. Leave the mixture in the bowl for about 1 hour to firm up, then roll into a log approx. 2 inches (5 cm) in diameter, wrap in parchment paper and place in fridge until firm.
7. Preheat oven to 350°F (180°C)
8. Cut the dough into 1/4 inch (1 cm) thick slices and place on the prepared trays 2 inches (5 cm) apart. Leave space because they spread.
9. Bake for 15 – 20 minutes until firm. Keep on tray until completely cool.
10. Sandwich the biscuits together with the cream

CREAM

1. Assemble the Ankarsrum with the plastic beater bowl and single wire cookie whisks.
2. Place the butter and confectioners' sugar in the plastic bowl and beat on speed three for 2 minutes or until smooth. Add the vanilla, milk and salt and continue for further minute, until smooth and creamy.

TIP: Unfilled cookies can be stored in airtight container for upto 5 days, however filled cookies are best eaten on the day they are filled.

M AND M COOKIE PIE

INGREDIENTS

113 grams soft butter (½ cup)
110 grams firmly packed brown sugar (½ cup)
4 grams vanilla extract (1 teaspoon)
1 large egg
250 grams all-purpose flour (2 cups)
2 grams baking soda (½ teaspoons)
100 grams M&M's or chocolate chips/chunks (½ cup) plus extra for decorating

METHOD

1. Preheat oven to 320°F (160°C)
2. Prepare a 9-inch (23cm) round cake tin by spraying well with cooking spray and lining with parchment paper.
3. Assemble the Ankarsrum with the plastic beater bowl and single wire cookie whisks.
4. Place the butter and sugar in the plastic beater bowl and beat at speed 3 for 2 minutes until well mixed.
5. Add vanilla extract and egg and continue to beat until soft and creamy. You may need to scrape down the bowl if the butter is sticking on the bottom.
6. Reduce to low speed and add the flour and baking soda. Beat on low just until cookie dough just starts to come together, then add the M&M's and chocolate chips. This should take less than a minute. It is important not to overbeat the dough because it causes strain on the beater gears.
7. Place dough into your prepared tin and spread out as evenly as possible. Press extra M&M's and chocolate chips on top. 8. Bake for 16-18 minutes or until golden brown on the edges. Try not to overcook as you want it soft and gooey in the middle. Leave to cool before slicing and serving.

TIP: If your brown sugar goes hard, place a slice of bread in the container overnight, it makes the bread go hard and the brown sugar soft!

GRAHAM CRACKERS

INGREDIENTS

220 grams all-purpose flour (1 ¾ cups)
140 grams wholemeal flour (1 ½ cups)
5 grams baking soda (1 teaspoon)
2 grams ground cinnamon (1 teaspoon)
1.5 grams kosher salt (½ teaspoon)
150 grams butter, soft (2/3 cup)
110 grams firmly packed brown sugar (½ cup)
85 grams honey (¼ cup)
30 grams water (2 tablespoons)

METHOD

1. Line 2 baking sheets with parchment paper
2. Assemble the Ankarsrum with the stainless steel bowl, scraper, and dough roller, with the roller against the edge.
3. Place butter, sugar, and honey in the Ankarsrum stainless steel bowl and mix at speed 3 for 3 minutes.
4. Reduce speed to low and add both flours, baking soda, cinnamon, and salt, and then increase speed back to speed 3 for a further 3 minutes or until the mixture looks like coarse sand. At this stage add the water starting at 1 tablespoon at a time until the dough comes together and forms a ball.
5. Remove the dough from the bowl, split it in half, and flatten each piece into a round disc. Wrap in plastic wrap and refrigerate for 30 minutes.
6. While the dough is chilling, Preheat oven to 350°F (180°C)
7. Remove the dough from the fridge and on a lightly floured work surface, roll it out until it is about ¼ inch (5mm) thick.
8. Using square cookie cutters or a sharp knife cut or press the dough into pieces and use a spatula to carefully transfer them to the prepared baking trays, making sure to leave a small gap between the cookies.
9. Bake for 10-12 minutes until they are lightly browned
10. Remove from the oven and allow to cool on the tray for 5 minutes, before transferring to a wire rack to finish cooling. The crackers will crisp up as they cool.

TIP: These can be store in an airtight container at room temperature for 10 days.

BROWNIE

INGREDIENTS

220 grams superfine sugar (1 cup)
2 eggs
150 grams butter, melted (2/3 cup)
65 grams dark cocoa (3/4 cup)
4 grams vanilla extract (1 teaspoon)
125 grams all-purpose flour (1 cup)
160 grams chocolate chunks roughly chopped (any type, milk, white, dark (1 cup)
100 grams raspberries (frozen or fresh) (1 cup)

METHOD

1. Preheat oven to 300°F (150°C)
2. Assemble the Ankarsrum with the plastic beater bowl and single wire cookie whisk
3. Prepare a 9-inch square baking tray (23cm), spray well with cooking spray and line with parchment paper.
4. Scatter the chocolate chunks on the bottom of the prepared tray and set aside.
5. Place eggs and sugar in the plastic beater bowl and beat for 2 minutes at speed 3 until creamy and pale. Reduce speed to low add melted butter, cocoa, and vanilla. Beat for a further 1 minute.
6. Add flour and beat until just combined.
7. Spread mixture into prepared tray and smooth out. You may need a hot knife or wet spatula because the mixture will be quite sticky.
8. Sprinkle raspberries on top, pushing some into the mixture, so they are in the middle, rather than the top.
9. Bake for 20-25 minutes. Don't overcook it, it needs to be slightly wobbly when it comes out of the oven

TIP:

Try this for an easy dessert
2 cups crème fraiche, 2 tablespoons sugar, 2 cups fresh or frozen berries, 1 slab of brownie (cut in cubes) In a bowl mix 1 cup of crème fraiche with the sugar and 1 cup of raspberries. Put 1/3 of the brownie in the base of 4 tall dessert glasses, then top with the crème fraiche berry mixture. Add 1/3 more cubed brownie, then the plain crème fraiche, sprinkle with another layer of cubed brownie and sprinkle with fresh berries.

LOUISE SLICE

INGREDIENTS

130 grams soft butter (½ cup plus 1 tablespoon)
150 grams granulated sugar (¾ cup)
2 egg yolks
4 grams vanilla extract (1 teaspoon)
185 grams all-purpose flour (1 ½ cups)
5 grams baking powder (1 teaspoon)
topping
1/2 cup raspberry jam (or any jam or curd)
2 egg whites
100 grams granulated sugar (½ cup)
4 grams vanilla extract (½ teaspoon)
170 grams shredded coconut (2 cups)

METHOD

1. Preheat oven to 320°F (160°C)
2. Spray an 8-inch (20cm) square baking pan with cooking spray. Line with parchment paper, letting an excess extend over the sides of the pan.
3. Assemble the Ankarsrum with the plastic beater bowl and single wire cookie whisk.
4. Place butter and sugar in the plastic beater bowl and beat at speed 3 for 2 minutes until creamy, scraping the bowl if butter is sticking to the bottom, then add the egg yolks and vanilla and continue speed 3, for a further 1 minute.
5. Reduce speed to low and add flour and baking powder for 1-2 minutes or until the mixture looks like large crumbs, don't overmix at this stage.
6. Press crumbly mixture into the prepared tin and bake for 15 minutes until pale and golden. While the base is cooking make topping.
7. Clean and assemble the Ankarsrum with the well clean and dry plastic beater bowl and balloon whisks. Place egg whites in the beater bowl and whisk at speed 6 until soft peaks appear, it will be about 2 minutes. Slow down to low and gradually add sugar and vanilla and whisk again at speed 6 for another minute. Stop the machine and fold in the coconut.
8. Remove the cooked base from the oven and while warm spread a thick layer of jam on the base, and then spoon the meringue mixture on top making small peaks.
9. Bake for 30 minutes or until crisp and golden. Cut while warm.

TIP: The bowl needs to be really clean and really dry to beat egg whites, If in doubt wipe the bowl with lemon juice or vinegar.

RASPBERRY AND MARSHMALLOW SLICE

INGREDIENTS

113 grams soft butter, (½ cup)
165 grams firmly packed brown sugar (¾ cup)
1 egg
4 grams vanilla extract (1 teaspoon)
125 grams all-purpose flour (1 cup)
44 grams cocoa (½ cup)
5 grams baking powder (1 teaspoon)
1.5 grams kosher salt (½ teaspoon)
Marshmallow
330g grams superfine sugar (1 ½ cups)
120 grams cold water (½ cup)
20 grams unflavored gelatin (7 teaspoons)
120 grams hot water (½ cup)
4 grams vanilla extract (1 teaspoon)
2 tablespoons freeze-dried raspberry powder or flavoring

METHOD

Brownie Base
1. Preheat oven to 340°F (170°C)
2. Assemble the Ankarsrum with the stainless steel bowl, scraper, and dough roller, with the roller against the edge.
3. Spray a 9-inch (23cm) square baking pan) with cooking spray. Line with parchment paper, letting an excess extend over the sides of the pan.
4. Place butter and sugar into the Ankarsrum stainless steel bowl and beat on speed 3 for 3 minutes. If the butter is sticking to the roller or dough knife, take the dough knife off for a couple of minutes and turn it up to full speed, then place the dough knife back on.
5. Add egg and vanilla and beat for 1 minute. Reduce speed to low and add cocoa, flour, baking powder and salt. Beat for a further 1 minute, or until combined. If some of the ingredients are not moving from the middle of the bowl slowly swing the dough roller into the middle for a few seconds to incorporate ingredients.
6. Press dough into the baking tin, it is a sticky dough so you may need wet hands, or a palette knife dipped in water. Try to get it as smooth as possible
7. Bake for 15 minutes or until a skewer inserted in the middle comes out clean. Set aside to cool.

Marshmallow
1. Assemble the Ankarsrum with the stainless steel bowl, scraper, and dough roller, with the roller against the edge.
2. Put sugar and cold water in the Ankarsrum stainless steel bowl and beat at speed 3 for 3 minutes.
3. While the sugar is beating, put the hot water in a small bowl, sprinkle gelatin over it and stir until dissolved. Check the gelatine mixture. If it has started setting, zap in the microwave for 30 seconds. It must be hot when it is added to the sugar mixture
4. Add gelatin to the sugar mixture and mix for 8- 10 minutes on high speed. It will eventually come together and be thick and creamy. About halfway through add vanilla and flavouring. It should be thick and smooth.
Spoon onto cooled brownie base and refrigerate until set. Cut with a hot knife.

BROOKIE

INGREDIENTS

BROWNIE LAYER
115 grams butter, melted (½ cup)
200 grams granulated sugar (1 cup)
4 grams vanilla extract (1 teaspoon)
2 grams salt (½ teaspoon)
2 eggs
88g cocoa powder (¾ cup)
30 grams all-purpose flour (¼ cup)
COOKIE LAYER
75 grams butter, melted (5 tablespoons)
110 grams firmly packed brown sugar (½ cup)
50 grams granulated sugar (¼ cup)
4 grams vanilla extract (1 teaspoon)
1 egg
125 grams all-purpose flour (1 cup)
2.5 grams teaspoon baking soda (½ teaspoon)
2 grams salt (½ teaspoon)
160 grams chocolate chips (1 cup)

METHOD

1. Preheat oven to 340°F (170°C).

2. Spray a 9-inch (23cm) square baking pan with cooking spray. Line with parchment paper, letting an excess extend over the sides of the pan.

3. To make the brownie layer: Assemble the Ankarsrum with the stainless steel bowl, scraper, and dough roller, with the roller against the edge.

4. Place the butter, sugar, vanilla, and salt in the Ankarsrum stainless steel bowl. Beat at speed 3 for 2 minutes until well mixed. Add the eggs one at time and continue for a further minute.

5. Reduce to speed 1, add cocoa powder and flour, and mix for approx. 1 minute or until just combined, careful not to over mix this stage. If some of the ingredients are not moving in the middle of the bowl slowly move the dough roller into the middle for a few seconds to incorporate ingredients.

6. Spoon the brownie mixture into the prepared container and spread evenly, then set aside. It may help to use wet hands to smooth the dough because it will be a sticky mixture.

7. To make the cookie layer: Assemble the Ankarsrum with the stainless steel bowl, scraper, and dough roller, with the roller against the edge.

8. Add the melted butter, brown sugar, and granulated sugar to the Ankarsrum stainless steel bowl and beat at speed 3 for 2 minutes until pale and creamy then add the vanilla and egg and beat well for a further 1 minute.

9. Reduce speed to low, add flour, baking soda, and salt, and beat until just mixed.

10. Finally add the chocolate chips and mix until just combined.

11. Take dollops of the cookie mixture and gently place it on top of the brownie layer, gently spreading each spoonful as you place it. The dough will be soft and sticky. You want the cookie dough to cover the entire brownie mixture as evenly as you can without pressing the dough into the brownie.

12 Cover the Brookie with foil and bake for 20 minutes, then remove the foil and bake for a further 20-30 minutes until the cookie layer is golden brown and or until a skewer inserted in the center of the brownie comes out clean.

13. Allow the Brookie to completely cool before removing it from the pan by lifting it with the parchment paper overhang.

CARAMEL SLICE

INGREDIENTS

125 grams all-purpose flour (1 cup)
5 grams baking powder (1 teaspoon)
220 grams firmly packed brown sugar (1 cup)
85 grams desiccated coconut (1 cup)
130 grams butter, melted (½ cup + 1 tablespoon)
1 can (14oz/397g) sweetened condensed milk
50 grams golden syrup (2 tablespoons)
28 grams butter; extra (2 tablespoons)
150 grams chocolate melts (mixture of white and dark) ½ cup
Handful of white chocolate bits

METHOD

1. Preheat oven to 350°F (180°C)
2. Assemble the Ankarsrum with the stainless steel bowl, scraper, and dough roller, with the roller against the edge.
3. Spray an 8-inch (20cm) square baking pan with cooking spray. Line with parchment paper, letting an excess extend over the sides of the pan.
4. Place flour, baking powder, brown sugar, and coconut into the Ankarsrum stainless steel bowl and mix on speed 3 for 1 minute until well mixed. Add melted butter and continue until well mixed and crumbly.
5. Tip out and press into the prepared pan.
6. Bake for 10 minutes, until lightly golden.
7. While the base is baking combine condensed milk, golden syrup, and butter (extra) in a microwave-safe bowl and cook in the microwave for around 2 minutes. Stop and stir vigorously every minute until slightly thickened.
8. When the base is golden, remove it from the oven and spread over the caramel mixture. Then bake for a further 10 minutes until dark golden. Cool.
9. Melt white and dark chocolate separately. Sprinkle white chocolate bits over the cooled slice, and then drizzle both types of melted chocolate over the top.
10. Refrigerate until set.

TIP: A slice tin 7 x 12 (18cm x 32cm) can replace an 8 or 9 inch square baking pan

MINT SLICE

INGREDIENTS

226 grams butter, room temperature, cubed (1 cup)
110 grams firmly packed brown sugar (½ cup)
50 grams granulated sugar (¼ cup)
1 egg
125 grams all-purpose flour (1 cup)
30 grams cocoa (⅓ cup)
Fresh mint cream filling
360 grams confectioners' sugar (3 cups)
42 grams butter, soft (3 tablespoons)
80 grams cream (⅓ cup)
8 grams pure peppermint essence (2 teaspoons)
1 bunch fresh mint leaves, finely chopped
Chocolate topping
100 g good-quality dark eating chocolate; (at least 50% cocoa)
80 grams cream (⅓ cup)
120 grams confectioners' sugar (1 cup)

METHOD

1. Preheat oven to 375°F (190°C)
2. Prepare a 9-inch square baking tray (23cm), spray well with cooking spray, and line it with parchment paper
3. Assemble the Ankarsrum with the stainless steel bowl, scraper, and dough roller, with the roller against the edge.
4. Place butter and both sugars in the Ankarsrum stainless steel bowl and beat on speed 3 for 3 minutes. Then add egg and continue for a further two minutes. If large clumps of butter are getting stuck on your scraper or roller, remove the scraper and beat on high for 2 minutes until the butter is creamed. Then place the scraper back onto the bowl to continue.
5. Reduce speed to low, add flour and cocoa, and continue for two minutes, until well mixed. If some of the ingredients are not moving in the middle of the bowl slowly move the dough roller into the middle for a few seconds to incorporate ingredients.
6. Spoon in prepared tin and even it out with a wet spatula. The mixture will be sticky.
7. Bake for 15 minutes and cool in the tin.
Mint Cream
8. Assemble the Ankarsrum with the beater bowl and single wire cookie whisk
9. Place icing sugar and butter into the beater bowl and beat at speed two for about 3 minutes. Add the peppermint essence and fresh mint, scrape the bottom of the bowl, and continue to beat for a further minute.
10. Spread over the cooled base and smooth out with a warm knife.
Chocolate Topping
In a medium bowl, melt chocolate and cream in a microwave with 1-minute bursts, stirring well between each burst, once it has melted add icing sugar and whisk until smooth.
Cool slightly and spread over the peppermint filling. Cover and place in the fridge for a least one hour.
Cut with a sharp knife. This slice needs to be kept in fridge.

LEMON CURD SHORTBREAD BAR

INGREDIENTS

226 grams soft butter, (1 cup)
135 grams granulated sugar (2/3 cup)
375 grams all-purpose flour (3 cups)
3 grams kosher salt (1 teaspoon)
4 grams vanilla extract (1 teaspoon)
500 grams lemon curd (2 cups)

METHOD

1. Preheat oven to 350°F (180°C)
2. Spray a 9-inch (23cm) square baking pan) with cooking spray. Line with parchment paper, letting an excess extend over the sides of the pan.
3. Assemble the Ankarsrum with the stainless steel bowl, scraper, and dough roller, with the roller against the edge.
4. Place butter, sugar, and vanilla in the Ankarsrum stainless steel bowl, and beat on speed 3 for 2 minutes, until pale and creamy, if large clumps of butter and sugar are getting stuck on your scraper or roller, remove the scraper and beat on high for 2 or 3 minutes until the butter and sugar are starting to become creamed. Then place the scraper back onto to bowl to continue. It will come together when the rest of the ingredients are added.
5. Reduce speed to low and add the flour and salt, increasing to 3 again, and continue beating for 2 more minutes until a dough has formed, if this is not happening add 1-2 tablespoons of water. At any time If some of the ingredients are not moving from the middle of the bowl slowly swing the dough roller into the middle for a few seconds to incorporate the ingredients.
6. Press 2/3 of the dough into the prepared pan and place the reserved 1/3 in the fridge to harden up.
7. Bake the base for 25 minutes or until lightly golden brown, and remove from the oven, and let it slightly cool in the pan.
8. Spread the lemon curd over the cooled base and crumble the chilled dough over the lemon curd. Return to the oven and bake for 30 minutes until golden brown. Cool in tin.

TIP: This book has weights in grams and cups for your convenience. However, if you want consistent results always weigh your ingredients.

GINGER CRUNCH

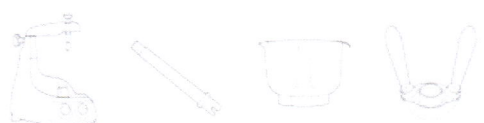

INGREDIENTS

130 grams soft butter, (½ cup plus 1 tablespoon)
100 grams granulated sugar (½ cup)
160 grams all-purpose flour (1 ¼ cups)
4 grams ground ginger (2 teaspoons)
5 grams baking powder (1 teaspoon)
Icing
90 grams butter (1/3 cup + 1 tablespoon) (extra)
180 grams confectioners' sugar (1 ½ cups)
21 grams golden syrup (1 tablespoon)
8 grams ground ginger (4 teaspoons)
Pistachios for decoration
Crystalized ginger for decoration

METHOD

1. Preheat oven to 350°F (180°C)
2. Spray a 9-inch (23cm) square baking pan) with cooking spray. Line with parchment paper, letting an excess extend over the sides of the pan.
3. Assemble the Ankarsrum with the plastic beater bowl and single wire cookie whisk
4. Place butter and sugar in the plastic beater bowl and mix on speed 3 for 3 minutes until pale and creamy.
5. Reduce speed to low and add baking powder and ginger. Then add flour and mix for a further minute on low for 1 minute or until just mixed. You don't want it to mix into a ball because it puts strain on the beater gears. If is not coming together you may need to scrape the bottom and sides with a rubber spatula if the butter is stuck to the bottom.
6. Press mixture into prepared pan and cook for 18-20min until pale golden.
7. While the base is cooking make the icing.

Icing
1. Place butter and golden syrup in the microwave for 1-2 minutes until melted. Add confectioners sugar and ginger and stir well. Spread icing onto the hot base, scatter chopped pistachio nuts and crystalized ginger on the warm icing (if using) cool slightly, and cut while warm.

TIP: The Single wire cookie whisks can be used for cookie dough, but only a single or half batch. If you want to double the recipe you must use the stainless bowl and roller. It is used for dough or batter that you don't want air to be incorporated. You can cream butter on high but never keep on high once you have added the flour.

SULTANA CAKE

INGREDIENTS

450 grams sultanas (2 ¼ cups)
226 grams butter, (1 cup)
3 eggs
300 grams granulated sugar (1 ½ cups)
500 grams all-purpose flour (4 cups)
15 grams baking powder (3 teaspoons)

METHOD

1. Preheat oven to 350°F (180°C)
2. Spray an 8-inch (20 cm) square baking pan with cooking spray. Line with parchment paper, letting an excess extend over the sides of the pan.
3. Assemble the Ankarsrum with the Ankarsrum stainless steel bowl, scraper, and dough roller, with the roller against the edge.
4. Boil sultanas for 8 minutes, then drain. Add butter and stir until melted and set aside.
5. Place eggs and sugar in the stainless bowl and beat at speed 4 for 2 minutes until creamy.
6. Move the roller to 1 inch from the edge and reduce speed to low. Add flour, baking powder, and the sultanas and beat for a further 2 minutes. If some of the ingredients are not moving in the middle of the bowl slowly move the dough roller into the middle for a few seconds to incorporate ingredients.
7. Bake for around 60 to 70 minutes or until a skewer inserted into the middle comes out clean.

TIP: The white scraper that comes with the Ankarsrum is designed to fit into the dough roller, and the curve is the same shape as the stainless bowl however do your self a big favour and also buy a cheap silicon jar spatcher .. they are the perfect width to scrap down your dough roller.

HUMMINGBIRD CAKE

INGREDIENTS

435 grams all-purpose flour (3 ½ cups)
3 grams kosher salt (1 teaspoon)
5 grams baking soda (1 teaspoon)
2 grams ground garam masala (1 teaspoon)
300 grams granulated sugar (1 ½ cups)
3 eggs
300 grams canola or vegetable oil (1 ¼ cups)
3 large ripe bananas; mashed (approx. 1 ½ cups)
60 grams walnuts roughly chopped (½ cup)
227 grams pineapple crushed (1 small 8 oz tin)
4 grams vanilla extract (1 teaspoon)

Icing
113 grams butter, soft (½ cup)
224 grams soft cream cheese (8oz) 1 packet
4 grams vanilla extract (1 teaspoon)
300 grams confectioners' sugar (2½ cups)

METHOD

1. Preheat oven to 350°F (180°C).
2. Spray an 8-inch (20cm) square or round baking pan with cooking spray. Line with parchment paper, letting an excess extend over the sides of the pan.
3. Assemble the Ankarsrum with the stainless steel bowl, scraper, and dough roller, with the roller against the edge.
4. Add flour, salt, baking soda, garam masala, and sugar into the Ankarsrum stainless steel bowl and mix on low speed for 1 minute. Add oil, then eggs, one at a time, and increase speed to 3 for 2 minutes. Then add mashed banana, chopped walnuts, crushed pineapple and vanilla. Reduce to speed one and mix for 1 minute until just mixed. If some of the ingredients are not moving from the middle of the bowl slowly swing the dough roller into the middle for a few seconds to incorporate ingredients.
5. Pour into prepared tin and cook for 45 minutes or until skewer inserted comes out clean.
6. Leave in the tin to cool. Wait until the cake is fully cooled before icing.
ICING
1. Assemble the Ankarsrum with the beater bowl and single wire cookie whisk.
2. Place butter in the plastic beater bowl and beat at speed 3 for 1 minute to make it smooth, then add soft cream cheese and vanilla and continue at speed 3 for 2 minutes until smooth and creamy.
3. Reduce to low speed and slowly add the confectioners' sugar, then increase speed to 3 again and beat for 1 to 2 minutes, until smooth. You may need to scrape the bottom of the bowl halfway through the mixing if you see some of the butter mixture stuck at the base.

CHOCOLATE CAKE

INGREDIENTS

250 grams all-purpose (2 cups)
350 grams granulated sugar (1 ¾ cup)
66 grams cocoa (¾ cup)
10 grams baking powder (2 teaspoons)
5 grams baking soda (1 teaspoon)
2 grams salt (½ teaspoon)
2 eggs
4 grams vanilla extract (1 teaspoon)
112 grams canola or vegetable oil (½ cup)
240 grams whole milk (1 cup)
240 grams boiling water (1 cup)

METHOD

1. Preheat oven to 320°F (160°C).
2. Prepare an 8-inch (20cm) cake tin square or round, by spraying well with cooking spray and lining it with parchment paper.
3. Assemble the Ankarsrum with the stainless steel bowl, scraper, and dough roller, with the roller against the edge.
4. Place the flour, sugar, cocoa, baking powder, baking soda, and salt in the Ankarsrum stainless steel bowl and beat at low speed for 1 minute until well mixed.
5. Add the eggs, vanilla, oil, and milk then increase to speed 3 and mix for 2-3 minutes.
6. Reduce speed and add the boiling water, then increase to speed 3 again and mix for 1 minute. If some of the ingredients are not moving in the middle of the bowl slowly move the dough roller into the middle for a few seconds to incorporate ingredients.
7. Pour into the prepared cake tin and bake for 45 minutes, or until a skewer inserted in the center comes out clean. This is a very runny mixture.

TIP: 9x13 inch cake tin is perfect for double quantity.

CARROT CAKE

INGREDIENTS

220 grams firmly packed brown sugar (1cup)
168 grams canola or vegetable oil (¾ cup)
2 eggs
4 grams ground cloves (2 teaspoons)
4 grams ground cinnamon (2 teaspoons)
300 grams grated carrot (2 heaped cups)
185 grams all-purpose flour (1 ½ cups)
5 grams baking powder (1 teaspoon)
5 grams baking soda (1 teaspoon)
120 grams walnuts chopped (1 cup)
Dried apricots, pumpkin seeds or extra nuts for decorations
Cream Cheese Icing
113 grams soft Butter (½ cup)
224 grams soft cream cheese (1 packet /8oz)
4 grams vanilla extract (1 teaspoon)
300 grams confectioners' sugar (2½ cups)

METHOD

1. Preheat oven to 320°F (160°C).
2. Assemble the Ankarsrum with the stainless steel bowl, scraper, and dough roller, with the roller against the edge.
3. Prepare an 8-inch (20 cm) cake tin round or square, by spraying well with cooking spray and lining it with parchment paper. (In the photo, I used mini loaf tins)
4. Place the brown sugar and oil into the Ankarsrum stainless steel bowl and beat on speed 3 for 2 minutes until well mixed. Add eggs, one at a time. Reduce the speed to low and add all the other ingredients (apart from the apricots and seeds for decorations) then increase speed again for 2 minutes, until well combined. If some of the ingredients are not moving from the middle of the bowl slowly swing the dough roller into the middle for a few seconds to incorporate ingredients.
5. Spoon into the prepared tin and bake for 1 hour or until a skewer inserted into the center comes out clean.
6. Leave in the tin for a few minutes before placing on a wire rack to cool. Wait until the cake is fully cooled before icing.
7. Ice with cream cheese icing and sprinkle with chopped nuts and dried apricots.
ICING
1. Assemble the Ankarsrum with the plastic beater bowl and single wire cookie whisk.
2. Place butter in the beater bowl and beat at speed 3 for 1 minute to make it smooth, then add soft cream cheese and vanilla and continue for 2 minutes until smooth and creamy.
Reduce to low speed and slowly add the confectioners' sugar, then increase speed back to 3 and beat for 1 to 2 minutes until smooth. You may need to scrape the bottom of the bowl halfway through the mixing if you see some of the butter mixture stuck to the base.

RASPBERRY AND APPLE CRUMBLE CAKE

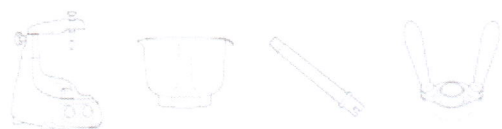

INGREDIENTS

112 grams soft butter (½ cup)
200 grams granulated sugar (1 cup)
4 grams vanilla extract (1 teaspoon)
2 eggs
10 grams baking powder (2 teaspoons)
310 grams all-purpose flour (2 ½ cups)
150 grams raspberries frozen (1 cup)
567 grams apple pie filling 1 can (20 oz)
For the crumble
112 grams butter, room temperature (½ cup)
125 grams all-purpose flour (1 cup)
75 grams firmly packed brown sugar (⅓ cup)
75 grams old fashion oats (¾ cup)

METHOD

1. Preheat oven to 350°F (180°C).
2. Assemble the Ankarsrum with the plastic beater bowl and single wire cookie whisk.
3. Spray a 9-inch (23cm) round baking pan with cooking spray. Line with parchment paper.
4. Make the crumble: In a medium bowl combine butter, flour, brown sugar, and oats and mix with your hands until the mix resembles fine crumbs and set aside.
5. Place the butter and sugar into the plastic beater bowl and beat at speed 2 for 1 minute until pale and fluffy.
6. Add the vanilla and then the eggs, one at a time, and beat until well combined. You may need to scrape the side and bottom of the bowl if the butter looks like it has stuck to the bottom of the bowl.
7. Return to speed 1 and add baking powder then flour and mix on low speed until just combined. Be careful not to overmix or the air will be pushed out of the cake, and it won't be fluffy.
8. Lightly press the cake batter into the prepared tin and spread it evenly with a spoon.
9. Sprinkle the frozen berries over the top of the cake batter and then spread a layer of canned apples over the berries.
10. Sprinkle the crumble layer evenly over the prepared cake.
11. Cook for 60 minutes or until a skewer inserted in the center comes out clean.
Allow the cake to rest in the tin for 30 minutes before transferring it to a wire rack to cool completely. Serve warm, or cold.

TIP:

Beater Gears
To assemble, place the black gear into the beater housing and snap the beater into place.
Be careful using the beater bowl and gears; if they have too much strain they can break.
Never overbeat the mixture, put chunky nuts or chocolate in it, or double a recipe.

RED VELVET BLACK FOREST CAKE

INGREDIENTS

130 grams soft butter, (½ cup plus 1 tablespoon)
135 grams granulated sugar (2/3 cup)
8 grams vanilla extract (2 teaspoons)
2 eggs, at room temperature
155 grams all-purpose flour (1 ¼ cups)
10 grams baking powder (2 teaspoons)
30 grams cocoa (⅓ cup)
240 grams whole buttermilk (1cup)
8 grams red food coloring (2 teaspoons)
Filling
2 x 14.5 OZ (415g) cans stoneless black cherries
480g cream (2 cups)
24 grams icing sugar (2 tablespoons)
13 grams vanilla extract (1 tablespoon)
50g dark chocolate (in a block)

METHOD

1. Preheat oven to 320°F (160°C)
2. Spray a 9-inch (23cm) round cake tin with cooking spray. Line the bottom with parchment paper.
3. Combine buttermilk and coloring in a jug and set aside
4. Assemble the Ankarsrum with the stainless steel bowl, scraper, and dough roller, with the roller against the edge.
5. Place butter, sugar, and vanilla in the Ankarsrum stainless steel bowl, and beat on speed 3 for 3 minutes, until smooth and creamy. Add eggs slowly, one at a time beating for 2 minutes until combined. (If large clumps of butter and sugar are getting stuck on your scraper or roller, remove the scraper and beat on high for 2 or 3 minutes until the butter and sugar are starting to become creamed.Then place the scraper back onto the bowl to continue. It will come together when the rest of the ingredients are added.)
6. Reduce speed to low and add flour, baking powder, and cocoa, alternately with the buttermilk mixture, and beat until just combined, around 1 minute.
7. Spread mixture into prepared pan and bake for 55 minutes or until a skewer inserted in the center comes out clean. Cool for 5 minutes then transfer to a wire rack to cool.
8. While the cake is baking, drain the cherries and reserve ¼ cup of the syrup.
9. Assemble the Ankarsrum with the beater bowl and balloon whisks. Place cream, vanilla, and confectioners' sugar in the beater bowl and beat on high for around 1.5 minutes, until peaks form. Be careful not to over-whip but keep in mind the cream needs to be quite firm.
10. When the cake is completely cooled, using a serrated knife cut the cake in half. Place one layer on a serving plate and brush with the reserved cherry juice.
11. Spread half the cream over half of the cake, cut half the cherries into chunks, and spread over the cream.
12. Place the other half of the cake on top of the cream and cherries, and place the remaining cream on top, Chill for one hour, and finally top with the remaining cherries and using a grater or vegetable peeler, grate chocolate over the cake.

CHOCOLATE CUPCAKES

INGREDIENTS

2 eggs
100 grams granulated sugar (½ cup)
110 grams packed brown sugar (½ cup)
75 grams vegetable oil (⅓ cup)
10 grams vanilla extract (2 teaspoons)
100 grams all-purpose flour (3/4 cup +1 tablespoon)
44 grams cocoa powder (½ cup)
4 grams instant coffee granules (2 teaspoons)
5 grams baking powder (1 teaspoon)
2 ½ grams baking soda (½ teaspoon)
3 grams salt (½ teaspoon)
115 grams buttermilk (½ cup)

METHOD

1. Preheat the oven to 350°F (180°C).
2. Assemble the Ankarsrum with the stainless steel bowl, scraper, and dough roller, with the roller against the edge.
3. Prepare a 6-cup Texan muffin tin, or standard 12-cup muffin tin with spray and cupcake liners.
4. Place eggs, granulated sugar, brown sugar, oil, and vanilla in the Ankarsrum stainless steel bowl and beat at speed 3 for 2 minutes until completely smooth.
5. Reduce speed and add all the dry ingredients and buttermilk into the bowl and mix on low until just combined. This should be less than a minute.
6. Pour the thin mixture into the cupcake liners, filling to halfway.
7. Bake for 20 minutes, or until a skewer inserted in the center comes out clean.
Note
If you don't have buttermilk, you can make your own by mixing 1 teaspoon of white vinegar or lemon juice to ½ cup of milk. Wait 5 minutes until it curdles.

ITALIAN MERINGUE

INGREDIENTS

- 220 grams superfine sugar (1 cup)
- 180 grams water (3/4 cup)
- 4 egg whites
- 3 grams lemon juice (1/2 teaspoon)

METHOD

1.Assemble the Ankarsrum with the plastic beater bowl and balloon whisks
2.Combine water and sugar in a saucepan and boil until 240°F (115°C)
Meanwhile, place egg whites and lemon juice in the plastic beater bowl and beat on high for 2 minutes until soft peaks form. Drizzle hot sugar syrup in a bowl and keep beating on high for 2 minutes or until stiff peaks form.

VANILLA CUPCAKES

INGREDIENTS

130 grams soft butter (½ cup plus 1 tablespoon)
4 grams vanilla extract (1 teaspoon)
165 grams Superfine sugar (¾ cup)
2 eggs
155 grams all-purpose flour (1 ¼ cups)
5 grams baking powder (1 teaspoon)
120 grams whole milk (½ cup)

METHOD

1. Preheat oven to 320°F (160°C)
2. Assemble the Ankarsrum with the plastic beater bowl and single wire cookie whisk
3. Prepare a 12-cup muffin pan with cupcake liners or 24 mini cupcakes
4. Place butter, sugar, and vanilla in the plastic beater bowl and beat on speed 3 for 2 minutes until light and fluffy.
5. Add egg, one at a time ensuring it is well mixed before adding the next one. This should take around one minute. Reduce speed to low and add flour, baking powder, and milk. Increase speed to 3 and beat for a further minute until well mixed. You may need to scrape the side and bottom of the bowl if the butter looks like it has stuck to the bottom of the bowl.
6. Spoon mixture into cupcake liners and bake for 10 minutes, or until a skewer inserted in the center comes out clean.
7. Cool completely before icing with American Butter Cream Icing.

AMERICAN BUTTER CREAM

INGREDIENTS

- 300 grams butter, soft (1 ⅓ cup)
- 300 grams confectioners' sugar (2 ½ cups)
- 4 grams vanilla extract (1 teaspoon)
- 15 grams whole milk (1 tablespoon) approx.
- Few drops food colouring

METHOD

1. Assemble the Ankarsrum with the stainless steel bowl, scraper, and dough roller, with the roller against the edge.
2. Place butter into the Ankarsrum stainless steel bowl and mix on high for 8 minutes. If large clumps of butter and sugar are getting stuck on your scraper or roller, remove the scraper for 2 or 3 minutes until the butter is starting to become creamed. Then place the scraper back onto the bowl to continue. It will come together when the rest of the ingredients are added.
3. Turn to low and add the icing sugar, once it is mixed turn back to high for approx. 2 minutes. Add milk, one teaspoon at a time if it is too stiff. When you want to stop mixing move the roller to the middle of the bowl for a moment. This makes the buttercream leave the edge of the bowl, so you have less mixture to scrape off the bowl.

MERINGUES

INGREDIENTS

6 room egg whites, room temperature, and fresh
310 grams superfine sugar (1 1/2 cups)
4 grams vanilla (1 teaspoon)
10 grams malt vinegar (2 teaspoons)
8 grams cornstarch (1 tablespoon)

METHOD

1. Preheat oven to 230°F (110°C)
2. Line 2 baking sheets with parchment paper.
3. Assemble the Ankarsrum with the stainless steel bowl, scraper, and dough roller, with the roller against the edge. Make sure your bowl is super clean, wipe with lemon juice or vinegar if you are not sure.
4. Place egg whites in the Ankarsrum stainless steel bowl and beat at full speed for 4 minutes until it is bubbly and starting to thicken.
5. Add vinegar, cornstarch, and vanilla, then slowly add sugar, one tablespoon at a time, and keep beating on full, it will take about 4 minutes. It will become smooth and shiny.
6. If some of the ingredients are not moving in the middle of the bowl slowly move the dough roller into the middle for a few seconds to incorporate ingredients.
7. Just before you finish, move the roller into the middle, and it will draw the meringue to the center, so there is less buildup on the edge.
8. You should be able to tip the bowl upside down and the meringue doesn't move
9. Put meringue in a piping bag and make nests, or piped meringues, or just plop large spoonfuls on a lined tray. Ensure all meringues on the tray are roughly the same size.
10. Cook for 1 hour, or until dry, leave in oven overnight to cool.

TIP:
Idea
Super simple deserts – especially for a crowd Eton Mess Break up a few meringues, mix in; 1 cup cream that has been whipped with 1 tsp vanilla extract and 2 tablespoons of confectioners' sugar, ½ cup Greek yogurt, 2 cups of frozen or fresh berries, and if you have them, a few marshmallows and a few scoops of ice-cream.

LIME PARFAIT WITH COCONUT CRUMBLE

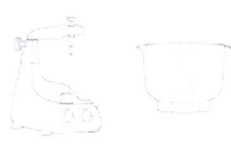  

INGREDIENTS

Parfait
300 grams cream (1 1/4 cups)
190 grams sweetened condensed milk (half a tin) (7oz)
9 grams lime zest (2 tablespoons)
15 grams lime juice (1 tablespoon)

Kaffir lime syrup
110 grams superfine sugar (1/2 cup)
60 grams water (¼ cup)
2 kaffir lime leaves, left whole
1 stalk lemongrass, bruised and roughly chopped
3cm knob fresh ginger, sliced
60 grams lime juice (1/4 cup)
Coconut crumble
60g thread coconut (1 cup)
50 grams granulated sugar (1/4 cup)
42 grams butter, chilled (3 tablespoons)
95 grams all-purpose flour (3/4 cup)
2 grams ground cinnamon (1 teaspoon)
1 gram ground nutmeg (1/2 teaspoon)
Pineapple salad
¼ pineapple, cut into small pieces
zest of 1 lime

METHOD

1. Assemble the Ankarsrum with the beater bowl and balloon whisks
2. Prepare six dariole molds or small ramekins by spraying them with oil and then wiping them out with a paper towel. You want them to just have a small amount of oil on them.
3. Place the cream and condensed milk together in the plastic beater bowl and whisk for 3 minutes on high until it forms stiff peaks. Fold through the lime juice and zest and taste to check that you can taste the lime.
4. Pour the mixture into the molds and place in the freezer for at least 6 hours or overnight, to set.
Kaffir lime syrup
1. Place the sugar, lemongrass, water, ginger, and kaffir lime leaves in a microwave-proof jug and heat until the sugar has dissolved. Add lime juice and set aside to cool and let flavors infuse. Place in fridge until ready to use
Coconut crumble
1. Preheat oven to 350°F (180°C)
2. Line 1 baking sheet with parchment paper.
3. Combine 50g of the coconut, sugar, butter, flour, cinnamon, and nutmeg in a food processor and blitz until combined. Transfer to the baking tray and press out flat.
4. Bake for 8-10 minutes, until golden. Remove from the oven and cool. Crush the crumble and add the remaining coconut. Keep in an airtight container until ready to use.
Pineapple salad
Place the pineapple and lime zest in a small bowl. Add a couple of teaspoons of the kaffir lime syrup and stir to combine.
To serve
Unmould the parfait and put it on a plate. Drizzle with the syrup, add a spoonful of the pineapple salad, and scatter over the coconut crumble.

PAVLOVA ROLL WITH SPICED CREAM

INGREDIENTS

6 egg whites
2.5 grams cream of tartar (½ teaspoon)
5 grams apple cider vinegar (1 teaspoon)
165 grams superfine sugar (¾ cup)
8 grams cornstarch (1 tablespoon)
25 grams flaked almonds (¼ cup)
250 grams cream fraiche (1 cup)
180 grams greek yogurt (¾ cup)
2 grams ground mixed spice (1 teaspoon)
12 grams icing sugar (1 tablespoon)
1 cup frozen Berries

METHOD

1. Preheat oven to 350°F (180°C).

2. Assemble the Ankarsrum with the plastic beater bowl and balloon whisks, make sure the bowl is super clean, wipe with lemon juice or vinegar if you are not sure.

3. Prepare a 10 x15 baking tray (38x26), spray well with cooking spray, and line with parchment paper.

4. Place egg whites, cream of tartar, and vinegar in the plastic beater bowl and beat on full speed for approx. 2 minutes until foamy with soft peaks starting to appear.

5. Slowly add sugar, a few tablespoons at a time, and keep beating for approx. 2 more minutes, combining the last 2 tablespoons of sugar with the cornstarch, and beat for a further minute.

6. Spread the meringue evenly on a lined baking sheet with a spatula, and sprinkle with flaked almonds.

7. Bake for 8 minutes at 350°F (180°C), then 20 minutes at 300°F (150°C)

8. Cool for 2 minutes then tip over onto a sheet of parchment paper lightly dusted in icing sugar. Peel off the top sheet.

9. Leave to cool for 15 minutes.

10. In a medium bowl whisk the creme fraiche, Greek yogurt, mixed spice, and second measure of confectioners' sugar until thick and smooth.

11. Spread cooked pavlova roll generously with the mixture and spread over berries.

12. Carefully lift the baking paper along the longest edge and roll the meringue up to enclose the filling. Wrap in foil and chill in the fridge for at least 2 hours. You can freeze it the day before by keeping it wrapped in foil and thaw in the fridge for 1 hour before serving slightly frozen. This pavlova roll works well with lemon curd, chocolate cream or berries, and unflavoured cream.

TIP: Only use the balloon whisks for things like egg white or cream, not creaming butter or thick frosting. They also whip very quickly, so don't step away from the mixer. The egg whites will break back down again if they are over-whipped.

STICKY DATE PUDDING

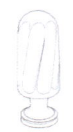

INGREDIENTS

190 grams chopped dates (1 cup)
5 grams baking soda (1 teaspoon)
120 grams boiling water (½ cup)
130 grams soft butter (½ cup + 1 tablespoon)
135 grams granulated sugar (2/3 cup)
2 eggs
185 grams all-purpose flour (1 ½ cups)
10 grams baking powder (2 teaspoons)

Caramel Sauce
175 grams firmly packed brown sugar (1 ¼ cup)
57 grams butter (¼ cup)
240 grams cream (1 cup)

METHOD

1. Preheat oven to 375°F (190°C)
2. I n a bowl sprinkle dates with baking soda and then pour the boiling water over them. Stir until soda is dissolved and allow to stand for 20 minutes.
3. Assemble the Ankarsrum with the stainless steel bowl, scraper, and dough roller, with the roller against the edge.
4. Prepare a baking dish (approx. 8 cups) by lightly spraying with cooking spray.
5. Place butter and sugar in the Ankarsrum stainless steel bowl, starting at low speed and gradually increasing speed to 3 for 4 minutes. Add one egg at a time and keep beating until light and fluffy.If large clumps of butter and sugar are getting stuck on your scraper or roller, remove the scraper and beat on high for 2 or 3 minutes until the butter and sugar is starting to become creamed. Then place the scraper back onto the bowl to continue. It will come together when the rest of the ingredients are added.
6. Reduce speed and add flour and baking powder, then dates and the water mixture. Increase speed to speed 3 again for about 4 minutes until well combined. If some of the ingredients are not moving in the middle of the bowl slowly move the dough roller into the middle for a few seconds to incorporate ingredients.
7. Pour into prepared baking dish and bake for 30-35 minutes, or until a skewer inserted into the middle comes out clean.

SAUCE
1. Combine all ingredients in a microwave-safe bowl and cook for 1 minute. Give it a brisk whisk then cook for a further minute (depending on the power of your microwave)
2. Pour a little sauce over the cooked pudding and put it back into the oven for a few minutes to allow it to soak and bubble until golden brown.
3. Serve the rest of the sauce with the pudding.

BLUEBERRY AND CHEESECAKE CUPCAKES

INGREDIENTS

100 grams granulated sugar (½ cup)
57 grams soft butter (¼ cup)
60 grams whole milk (¼ cup)
1 egg
4 grams vanilla extract (1 teaspoon)
5 grams baking powder (1 teaspoon)
185 grams all-purpose flour (1 ½ cups)

For the Cheesecake Filling:
1 package (8 oz) 225 grams cream cheese, softened
60 grams sour cream (¼ cup)
50 grams white chocolate, melted (⅓ cup)
50 grams granulated sugar (¼ cup)
1 egg
75 grams fresh or frozen blueberries (½ cup)
For the Topping:
Fresh blueberries
Blueberry jam
240 grams cream (1 cup)
4 grams vanilla extract (1 teaspoon)
12 grams confectioners' sugar (1 tablespoon)

METHOD

For the Cupcake Base:
1. Preheat oven to 350°F (175°C). Line 12 muffin tin with cupcake liners.
2. Assemble the Ankarsrum with the plastic beater bowl and single wire cookie whisk
3. Place butter and sugar in the plastic beater bowl and beat on speed 3 for 3 minutes or until light and fluffy. Add egg and vanilla and continue beating for 1 minute.
4. Reduce speed to 1 and add flour and baking powder alternately with milk until just combined, this will take less than one minute.
5. Divide the batter among the cupcake liners, filling each about one-third full.
For the cheesecake filling:
6. Assemble the Ankarsrum with the beater bowl and single wire cookie whisk
7. Add cream cheese, sour cream, melted white chocolate, and sugar to the plastic beater bowl and beat on speed 2 for 3 minutes or until smooth. Add egg and beat until well combined. Remove from the machine and fold in the blueberries.
8. Spoon the cheesecake mixture over the base, filling each liner nearly to the top.
9. Bake for 22-25 minutes, or until set. Allow to cool in the pan for 10 minutes, then remove to a wire rack to cool completely.
Topping:
10. Assemble the Ankarsrum with the plastic beater bowl and balloon whisk, place cream, confectioners' sugar, and vanilla in bowl and beat for 2 minutes until soft peaks appear
11. Top each cupcake with whipped cream, a spoonful of blueberry jam, and a few fresh blueberries.

LEMON AND LIME TART

INGREDIENTS

3 eggs
165 grams Superfine sugar (3/4 cup)
120 grams cream (1/2 cup)
60 grams lemon juice (1/4 cup)
30 grams lime juice (2 tablespoons)
2 grams lemon zest (1 teaspoon)
2 grams lime zest (1 teaspoon)

Shortcrust pastry (see page)

METHOD

1. Assemble the Ankarsrum with the plastic beater bowl and single wire cookie whisk
2. Prepare a 9 inch (23cm) flan dish by spraying well with cooking spray
3. Roll out the pastry and carefully lift it onto the prepared dish, gently pressing into the edges to fit well, but not stretching it, because this will make it shrink. Trim pastry from edges if necessary.
4. Rest in the fridge for 30 minutes minimum
5. Preheat oven to 350°F (180°C)
6. Blind bake tart, by filling parchment paper, or microwave-safe clingwrap with rice or baking beans, and bake for 10 minutes. Remove beans and cook for a further 10 minutes.
7. While blind baking, make the filling. Place the eggs and sugar in the plastic beater bowl and beat on speed 6 for 2 minutes until well combined, then add cream, both juices, and both zests. Continue beating for 1 minute. You may need to give the bottom a quick scrap if sugar is not moving from the bottom.
8. Pour mixture into the semi-cooked flan base and cook for a further 20 minutes or until just set.
9. Serve warm or cold.

TIP: Microwave safe clingwrap works great when you blind bake a tart base. It's much easier than parchment paper. Be generous with the clingwrap, and lay it on the uncooked tart base, then fill it up with rice, bean, or baking beans, and scrunch it up so you have a way to just lift it out while it is hot.

PLUM CHEESECAKE

INGREDIENTS

250 grams crushed cookies (2 cups)
90 grams butter, soft (⅓ cup plus 1 tablespoon)
240g cream (1 cup)
1 packet cream cheese, room temperature (226 grams, 8oz)
60 grams confectioners' sugar (½ cup)
1 lemon; zest
30 grams lemon juice (2 tablespoons)
4 grams vanilla extract (1 teaspoon)
2 cans (15oz) (425g) black plums (or black doris plums)
60 grams very hot water (¼ cup)
24 grams granulated sugar (2 tablespoons)
18 grams unflavored gelatin (6 teaspoons)

METHOD

1. Prepare a round 9-inch (22cm) spring form pan by lining and spraying lightly with cooking spray, or individual containers (pictured).
2. Place crushed cookies and butter in a bowl and mix well.
3. Press the crumb mixture into the prepared pan, and place in the fridge for 20 minutes.
4. Assemble the Ankarsrum with the plastic beater bowl and balloon whisks.
5. Place cream in the plastic beater bowl and beat on high for 1 ½ to 2 minutes until firm peaks appear. It won't take long! When whipping cream, you need to go by sight rather than timing, so don't move far away from the mixer! Spoon into a bowl and set aside
6. Assemble the Ankarsrum with the plastic beater bowl and single wire cookie whisk
7. Beat the soft cream cheese on speed 6 for 2 minutes until smooth and creamy. Scrap the bottom of the bowl with a rubber spatula then reduce the speed to low and add confectioners' sugar, lemon zest, lemon juice, and vanilla, then increase speed again to 6 for 3 minutes until thick and creamy. Fold in whipped cream.
8. Spread the cream cheese mixture on the crumb base and put it in the fridge again for 30 minutes.
9. Assemble the Ankarsrum with the stainless steel bowl, dough knife, and dough roller.
10. Remove stones from plums, place in Ankarsrum stainless steel bowl, and mix at 6 for 3 minutes until well mixed.
11. While plums are mixing, place hot water, sugar, and gelatin in a small bowl and mix until gelatin is dissolved.
12. Add gelatin to the plum mixture, then beat for a further minute.
13. Pour plum mixture on top of cheesecake and refrigerate for at least 3 hours.

CHOUX PASTRY

INGREDIENTS

75 grams butter (⅓ cup)
240 grams water (1 cup)
12 grams granulated sugar (1 tablespoon)
125 grams all-purpose flour (1 cup)
4 eggs

METHOD

1. Preheat oven to 410°F (210°C).
2. Line 2 baking sheets with parchment paper.
3. Assemble the Ankarsrum with the stainless steel bowl, scraper, and dough roller, with the roller against the edge.
4. Place water, butter, and sugar in a saucepan and bring to the boil. Once boiling, take off the heat and stir in flour, beating vigorously, until it turns into a pasty ball.
5. Place the flour mixture into the Ankarsrum stainless steel bowl and beat at speed 6 for 1 minute to slightly cool the mixture.
6. Then, add one egg at a time, ensuring each egg is well mixed before adding the next one.
7. Turn up to speed 6 and beat for 4 minutes until glossy.
8. Place the mixture into a piping bag and pipe depending on what you are making. (see below)
9. Bake at 410 °F (210°C) for 10 minutes, turn down the heat to 350°F (180°C) and cook for a further 10 minutes. Poke/Slit small holes into the side of the puffs and return to the oven for 10 more minutes.
10. Turn off the oven and leave puffs in the oven to dry.

Piping
Cream Puffs 1.5 inches (4cm) spirals
Eclairs: 5 inches x 1 inch tubes (12cm x 2.5cm)
Mini Eclairs: 3 inches x 1 inch (8cm x 2cm) tubes
Profiteroles: 2 inches (5 cm) spirals

Fill with cream or cream diplomat (recipe on next page)
Drizzle with chocolate ganache: 100 grams chocolate and ½ cup cream – zap in microwave in bursts and stir until smooth.

CRAQUELIN

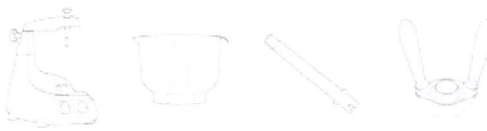

INGREDIENTS

112 grams butter, room temperature (½ cup)
125 grams all-purpose flour (1 cup)
110 grams firmly packed brown sugar (½ cup)
2 grams vanilla extract (½ teaspoon)
To be combined with the Choux pastry recipe

METHOD

1. Assemble the Ankarsrum with the plastic beater bowl and single wire cookie whisk.
2. Add all ingredients into the plastic beater bowl and beat at low speed for a minute, or until well mixed and crumbly. Do not mix until it's a ball because it will cause strain on your plastic beater gears.
3. Either squish the dough together with your hands while in the bowl or tip it onto the bench and bring it together into a ball.
4. Turn the dough onto a large piece of parchment paper and place another sheet of parchment on top.
5. Roll out to 2mm in thickness. It will be about the size of an A4 piece of paper.
6. Place dough flat in the freezer for a minimum of 30 minutes or until hard.
7. Make choux pastry as per instructions.
8. Line two baking sheets with parchment paper.
9. When you are ready to pipe the choux, take the craquelin out of the freezer and cut circles with a 2-inch (5cm) round cookie cutter. Pipe the choux into approx. ½inch (4cm) mounds, and immediately after you have piped the choux on the tray place one disk of craquelin carefully on the piped choux. Work as quickly as you can.
10. Bake immediately in a hot oven at 390°F (200°C) for 10 minutes.
11. Reduce heat to 350°F (180°C) and bake for a further 10 minutes.
12. Open the oven and make a small slit carefully on the side of the choux.
13. Cook for a further 10 minutes, then turn the oven off and let them dry out.
14. Either slice in half and fill or make a small hole in the bottom and pipe in whipped cream or crème diplomat. These are stunning and easy.

Crème Patisserie
320 grams warm whole milk (1 ⅓ cup)
4 grams vanilla extract (1 teaspoon)
55 grams Superfine sugar (¼ cup)
2 eggs
24 grams cornstarch (3 tablespoons)

1.Combine milk and vanilla in a microwave jug and heat until hot, but not boiling.
2.In another bowl, beat together the sugar, eggs, and cornstarch until it's a thick paste.
3.Add half the hot milk to the egg mixture to temper it and mix well, then pour that mixture back into the remaining milk. Cook in the microwave in 1-minute bursts for about 6 minutes (depending on your microwave) stirring each time until thick. Place clear wrap on the top of the mixture (to stop getting a film over it) and cool completely before using.

Crème Diplomat
240 grams cream (1 cup)
1 cup cream patisserie
Whip cream until stiff peaks appear.
Beat chilled cream patisserie until smooth. Fold whipped cream into the patisserie. Refrigerate for up to 3 days.

SWEET SHORTCRUST PASTRY

INGREDIENTS

250 grams all-purpose (2 cups)
40 grams confectioners' sugar (⅓ cup)
130 grams soft butter (½ cup plus 1 tablespoon)
1 egg
15 grams icy cold water (1 tablespoon)

METHOD

1. Assemble the Ankarsrum with the plastic beater bowl and single wire cookie whisk.
2. Place flour, confectioners' sugar, and then cubed butter in the plastic beater bowl and mix at speed 3 for 1 minute until it resembles fine breadcrumbs.   Scrap butter off the bottom of the bowl.
3. Reduce the speed to 1, add egg and icy water, and continue to mix only until it resembles large breadcrumbs. (For less than one minute.)You need to watch it and don't beat into a ball. If it overbeats it will be tough. Add more water, just a teaspoon at a time if it's not coming together.
4. While the dough is in the plastic bowl, squeeze the dough with your hands to make it form a lump.
5. Tip onto a lightly floured bench, bring together into a ball, and knead for 30 seconds, then press into a thick disk about 1 inch high
6. Wrap in cling wrap and chill for a minimum of 1 hour.
7. Roll out as required. If you are making a tart. Line the tart and chill again for an hour, or cover and freeze until you need it.

TIPS FOR PASTRY:

This is a handy recipe and can be used for any tart.
The trick is to have icy water, not just cold.
- Place some ice cubes into a glass of water to make it icy cold.
- Rest rest and rest.
- Don't overbeat – it will become tough.
- Don't try and stretch or push the dough into the flan dish – that will make it shrink, just be gentle.
- Always chill before baking it.

CREME BRULEE

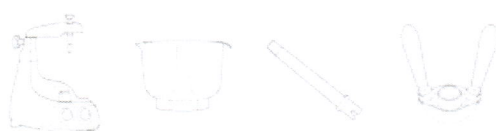

INGREDIENTS

240 grams cream (1 cup)
2 grams vanilla extract (½ teaspoon)
3 egg yolks
40 grams superfine sugar (⅓ cup)
50 grams granulated sugar (¼ cup) approx.

METHOD

1. Lightly grease 6 ramekins.
2. Assemble the Ankarsrum with the plastic beater bowl and single wire cookie whisk
3. Heat cream and vanilla in a small saucepan or microwave but don't let it come to a boil.
4. While the cream is heating, place egg yolks and superfine sugar into the plastic beater bowl and beat at speed 6 for 1 minute. You may need to stop and scrape down sugar.
5. Reduce speed to low and slowly pour in the hot cream, then increase speed to 3 for 2 minutes.
6. Strain the mixture and pour it into 6 ramekins.
7. Place ramekins into a deepish ovenproof dish and place it in the oven.Pour water into the dish so it is halfway up the sides of the ramekins.
8. Bake for 30 minutes at 250°F (120°C) then turn and bake for another 20 minutes.They will be set in the middle if fully cooked.
9. Lightly cover in granulated sugar and burn with a gas torch or place under the grill until the sugar melts and caramelizes.

TIP: This is a good recipe to use up the egg yolks from other recipes

BERRY WHIP

INGREDIENTS

1 can berries (425 grams 15oz)
(boysenberries, raspberries, blackberries)
1 packet (80 grams 3 oz) red jelly crystals
240 grams cream (1 cup)

METHOD

1. Assemble the Ankarsrum with the plastic beater bowl and balloon whisks
2. Drain juice from berries and place juice in a microwave-safe bowl and boysenberries in another large bowl.
3. Add jelly crystals to the juice and heat in the microwave until the jelly has dissolved, around 1-2 minutes, and stir well.
4. Place cream in the plastic beater bowl and beat for 1 to 2 minutes, until soft peaks appear, watching carefully that you don't overbeat
5. Add juice mixture and whipped cream to the boysenberries and fold together carefully.
6. Place in fridge for a minimum of 4 hours.

This can be chilled in individual dishes (like the photo) or one large dish.

TIP: The plastic beater bowl is also available in stainless steel, however, for this book, I have referred to it as the plastic bowl because that is the one that comes standard with the machine.
You can put boiling water in the plastic beater bowl.
The handle faces you and the pouring spout faces the machine

BANANA BREAD WITH PASSION FRUIT ICING

INGREDIENTS

150 grams butter, melted (2/3 cup)
110 grams firmly packed brown sugar (½ cup)
85 grams golden syrup (¼ cup)
2 eggs
300 grams mashed banana (1 ½ cups) approx. 3
375 grams all-purpose flour (3 cups)
15 grams baking powder (3 teaspoons)
8 grams vanilla extract (2 teaspoons)
2 grams ground cinnamon (1 teaspoon)
120 grams whole milk (½ cup)

Passionfruit icing
200 grams confectioners' sugar (1 2/3 cups)
14 grams soft butter (1 tablespoon)
60ml passionfruit pulp (¼ cup)
15 grams water (1 tablespoon)

METHOD

1. Preheat oven to 320°F (160°C)
2. Prepare a 9 x 5 inch loaf tin (22cm x 12cm). Spray well with cooking spray and line with parchment paper, extending paper over the sides.
3. Assemble the Ankarsrum with the stainless steel bowl, dough knife, and dough roller.
4. Place butter and brown sugar in the Ankarsrum stainless steel bowl and beat at speed 6 for 1 minute until well mixed. Reduce speed to low add egg, banana, and golden syrup, and continue beating for 1 minute.
5. Continue on low speed while you add flour, baking powder, vanilla, cinnamon, and milk, then increase speed again to 3 and beat until well combined, around 1 minute.
6. Spoon mixture into prepared pan; smooth the surface.
At any time if some of the ingredients are not moving in the middle of the bowl slowly move the dough roller into the middle for a few seconds to incorporate the ingredients.
7. Bake for 1 hour (cover loosely with foil if it starts to over-brown) or until a skewer inserted in the center comes out clean. Leave cake in pan for 10 minutes before transferring to a wire rack to cool.
8. Meanwhile, make the Passionfruit icing.
Place icing sugar, butter, pulp and water in a small microwave-safe bowl and heat in the microwave in 30-second bursts. Stir between each burst and continue until the icing is spreadable.
9. Spread on cooled loaf.

DATE LOAF

INGREDIENTS

300 grams pitted dates chopped (1 ½ cups)
180 grams water (¾ cup)
1 orange; zest and juice
120 grams whole milk (½ cup)
150 grams soft butter (2/3 cup)
165 grams firmly packed brown sugar (¾ cup)
2 eggs
8 grams vanilla extract (2 teaspoons)
250 grams all-purpose (2 cups)
10 grams baking powder (2 teaspoons)
5 grams baking soda (1 teaspoon)
2 grams ground cinnamon (1 teaspoon)
2 grams ground mixed spice (1 teaspoon)
2 grams ground ginger (1 teaspoon)

METHOD

1. Preheat oven to 320°F (160°C)
2. Add the dates to a small saucepan with the water, orange zest, and juice and simmer for 5-10 minutes until most of the liquid has evaporated. Take off the heat and stir in the milk, set aside, and leave to cool to room temperature.
3. Assemble the Ankarsrum with the stainless steel bowl, scraper, and dough roller, with the roller against the edge.
4. Prepare a 9 x 5 inch loaf tin (22cmx 12cm) spray well with cooking spray and line with parchment paper, letting the excess extend over the sides of the pan.
5. Place butter and sugar in the Ankarsrum stainless steel bowl and beat on speed 3 for 2 minutes until pale and fluffy. If large clumps of butter are getting stuck on your scraper or roller, remove the scraper and beat on high for 2 minutes until the butter is creamed. Then place the scraper back onto the bowl to continue.
6. Add the eggs and vanilla and beat for a further minute.
7. Reduce to low speed and add the flour, baking powder, baking soda, cinnamon, mixed spice and ginger and increase speed to 3 again and continue mixing for a further minute. Add the cooled date mixture to the bowl and mix until just combined, around 1 minute. If some of the ingredients are not moving from the middle of the bowl slowly swing the dough roller into the middle for a few seconds to incorporate ingredients.
8. Spoon the mixture into the tin and smooth out the top.
9. Bake for 1 hour 10 minutes, or until a skewer inserted in the center comes out clean. Remove from the oven and cool for 10-15 minutes in the tin – then finish cooling on a wire rack.

TIP: Serve with lashings of butter!

GINGERBREAD LOAF

INGREDIENTS

150 grams butter (2/3 cup)
85 grams golden syrup (1/4 cup)
250 grams all-purpose flour (2 cups)
5 grams baking powder (1 teaspoon)
5 grams baking soda (1 teaspoon)
2 grams ground cinnamon (1 teaspoon)
8 grams ground ginger (4 teaspoons)
3 grams kosher salt (1 teaspoon)
220 grams firmly packed brown sugar (1 cup)
1 egg
240 grams whole milk (1cup)
1 tablespoon brown sugar - extra for topping

METHOD

1. Preheat oven to 340°F (170°C)
2. Prepare a 9 x 5 inch loaf tin (22cmx 12cm) spray well with cooking spray and line with parchment paper, extending paper over the sides.
3. Assemble the Ankarsrum with the stainless steel bowl, scraper, and dough roller, with the roller against the edge.
4. Melt butter and golden syrup in the microwave and stir to combine. Set aside.
5. Place the flour, baking powder, baking soda, cinnamon, ginger, salt, and brown sugar in the Ankarsrum stainless steel bowl and beat at speed 1 for 1 minute to thoroughly mix.
6. Add butter and golden syrup mixture, egg, and milk, and increase to speed 3 for 3 minutes until well combined. At any time, some of the ingredients are not moving in the middle of the bowl slowly move the dough roller into the middle for a few seconds to incorporate the ingredients.
7. Pour the mixture into the loaf tin.
8. Crumble over 1 tablespoon of brown sugar.
9. Bake for 1 hour or until a skewer inserted into the middle comes out clean.

TIP: If you use your phone or iPad in the kitchen, cover it with clingwrap. It saves the flour from getting into it but you can still use the touchscreen

BLUEBERRY AND LEMON LOAF

INGREDIENTS

150 grams soft butter (2/3 cup)
200 grams granulated sugar (1 cup)
4 grams lemon zest (2 teaspoons)
120 grams lemon juice (½ cup)
2 eggs
280 grams all-purpose flour (2 ¼ cups)
5 grams baking powder (1 teaspoon)
5 grams baking soda (1 teaspoon)
130 grams blueberries (fresh or frozen) (¾ cup)

Icing
120 grams confectioners' sugar (1 cup)
30 grams water (2 tablespoons)
2 grams lemon zest (1 teaspoons)
30 grams lemon juice (2 tablespoons)
Coloring optional

METHOD

1. Preheat oven to 350°F (180°C)
2. Assemble the Ankarsrum with the stainless steel bowl, scraper, and dough roller, with the roller against the edge.
3. Spray a 9 x 5 inch loaf tin (22cm x 12cm) with baking spray. Line with parchment paper, letting an excess extend over the sides of the pan.
4. Place butter and sugar in the Ankarsrum stainless steel bowl and beat at speed 3 for 2 minutes until pale and creamy. Add lemon juice, zest and then eggs and beat for a further 1 minute. If large clumps of butter and sugar are getting stuck on your scraper or roller, remove the scraper and beat on high for 2 or 3 minutes until the butter and sugar are starting to become creamed.Then place the scraper back onto the bowl to continue. It will come together when the rest of the ingredients are added.
5. Reduce speed to low and add flour, baking powder, and baking soda. Beat together until just combined, less than one minute. At any time if some of the ingredients are not moving from the middle of the bowl slowly swing the dough roller into the middle for a few seconds to incorporate the ingredients.
6. Pour a third of the mixture into the prepared loaf tin, and scatter half of the blueberries over the batter. Repeat with the next third of the mixture and the rest of the blueberries. Then cover with the remaining loaf mixture and smooth the top.
7. Bake for 50-60 minutes or until a skewer inserted in the center comes out clean.
8. Icing: Place the icing sugar, lemon zest, and juice in a bowl and stir well, using 1-2 tsp of boiling water to get the right consistency, and drizzle the icing over the loaf once it has cooled. Once the icing has set slice and serve.

FRESH GINGER AND PEAR LOAF

INGREDIENTS

200 grams butter, (1 cup less 2 tablespoons)
150 grams firmly packed brown sugar (2/3 cup)
85 grams golden syrup (¼ cup)
4 grams vanilla extract (1 teaspoon)
120 grams whole milk (½ cup)
3 tablespoons finely grated fresh ginger
2 eggs
2 medium pears, fresh or canned
250 grams all-purpose (2 cups)
10 grams ground cinnamon (5 teaspoons)
10 grams baking powder (2 teaspoons)
2½ grams baking soda (½ teaspoon)
4 grams ground cardamon (2 teaspoons)
3 grams kosher salt (1 teaspoon)

METHOD

1. Preheat oven to 300°F (150°C)
2. Prepare a 9 x 5 inch loaf tin (22cm x 12cm) spray well with cooking spray and line with parchment paper, extending paper over the sides.
3. Assemble the Ankarsrum with the stainless steel bowl, scraper, and dough roller, with the roller against the edge.
4. Peel and thinly slice the pears and set aside.
5. Melt butter, sugar, and golden syrup in the microwave, leave to cool slightly then add the milk, vanilla, fresh ginger, and eggs. Whisk to combine.
6. Place the flour, ground ginger, baking powder, baking soda, cardamom, and salt in the Ankarsrum stainless steel bowl and mix at speed 1 for 1 minute.
7. Add butter mixture and increase speed to 3 for 3 minutes, until well combined.
At any time if some of the ingredients are not moving in the middle of the bowl slowly move the dough roller into the middle for a few seconds to incorporate the ingredients.
8. Remove the bowl from the machine, fold half the sliced pears through the loaf batter, and scrape into the prepared loaf tin. Arrange the remaining slices on the top of the batter, more on the sides rather than the middle, so that it can still rise.
9. Bake in the preheated oven for 70 minutes, or until a skewer inserted into the center comes out clean. Cool in the tin for 15 minutes or so, then turn out onto a cooling rack.

TIP: In Ankarsrum recipes the timer is sometimes referred to a time. 1 O'clock is speed 1, 6 o'clock is speed 6

LEMON CURD

INGREDIENTS

6 egg yolks
165 grams Superfine sugar (¾ cup)
180 grams lemon juice (¾ cup)
113 grams butter, melted (½ cup)

METHOD

1. Assemble the Ankarsrum with the plastic beater bowl and balloon whisks
2. Place all ingredients in the plastic beater bowl, place the white lid on, and turn on the highest speed for 3 minutes.
3. Pour into a microwave-proof jug and blitz in the microwave in 1-minute increments four or five times (depending on the power of the microwave), vigorously whisking for 30 seconds between each burst. Or place in a saucepan and boil, stirring continuously.
4. Pour into a jar with a lid and place in the fridge to firm up. The curd will still appear a little runny but will thicken up in the fridge.

TIP: The White Lid is great for covering the plastic beater bowl when you have liquids that you need to beat at full speed. It is also great to cover the stainless steel bowl when you are proving dough

CARAMEL POPCORN

INGREDIENTS

50 grams popcorn kernels (¼ cup)
220 grams superfine sugar (1 cup)
90 grams butter, soft (⅓ cup + 1 tablespoon)
12 grams sea salt (2 teaspoons)

METHOD

1. Preheat oven to 275°F (140°C).
2. Prepare a large baking pan with edges by spraying it with oil and lining with parchment paper.
3. Place popcorn in a paper bag and cook in the microwave for up to 2 minutes, depending on your microwave, (or whatever method you prefer to pop it), and spread it on the baking tray.
4. Prep Caramel: Place sugar in a medium saucepan, melt on medium heat, and boil until it darkens slightly. When amber add butter and whisk until caramel is formed, Pour over popcorn.
5. Place in oven for 5 minutes, stir, and repeat every 5 minutes until all popcorn has layers on it.
6. Remove from oven and sprinkle with salt.

TIP: Use in popcorn and pecan cookies or just snack on it. Store in an airtight container for 4 weeks.

CHUNKY HUMMUS

INGREDIENTS

1 can chickpeas (15.5oz)
2 cloves garlic clove; crushed
¼ cup lemon juice
¼ cup tahini
¼ cup olive oil
pinch of salt

METHOD

1. Assemble the Ankarsrum with the stainless steel bowl, scraper, and dough roller, with the roller against the edge.
2. Drain and rinse the chickpeas.
3. Place the chickpeas in the Ankarsrum stainless steel bowl and beat at speed 6 for 5 minutes or until they have broken down.
4. Reduce speed to low and add garlic, lemon juice, tahini, olive oil, and salt. Increase speed to 6 again for 2 more minutes until well mixed.
5. Add water, a tablespoon at a time if it is too thick.

TIP: This is quite chunky, if you prefer smoother use your blender.

DOG COOKIES

INGREDIENTS

300 grams wholemeal flour (2½ cups)
1 large egg
220 grams peanut butter (1 cup) (see note below)
240 grams water (1 cup)
44 grams honey (2 tablespoons)
FOR THE FROSTING
35 grams peanut butter (2 tablespoons)
22 grams honey (1 tablespoon)
32 grams cornstarch (¼cup)
45 grams hot water (4 tablespoons)

METHOD

1. Preheat oven to 350°F (180°C).
2. Line 2 baking sheets with parchment paper.
3. Assemble the Ankarsrum with the stainless steel bowl, scraper, and dough roller, with the roller secured 1 inch from the edge.
4. Place the flour and egg into the Ankarsrum stainless steel bowl and mix at low speed for one minute, then add the peanut butter, water, and honey, and mix on speed 2 for 3 minutes until you have a stiff dough. The dough becomes very firm and sticky.
5. On a lightly floured surface, roll out the dough about ½-inch thick (13mm) and either cut or use a cookie cutter to make shapes. The cookies don't spread, so you can have lots of options with your cutters.
6. Bake for 18-20 minutes, until golden. Once done, set aside to cool.
7. To make the frosting, combine the peanut butter and honey in a microwavable bowl, and heat in the microwave in 30-second increments, stirring in between, until melted.
8. Add the melted peanut butter mixture to the cornstarch and stir until just combined.
9. Slowly add in the water 1 tablespoon at a time until you have reached the consistency that you would like. For a thinner frosting, add more water.
10. Add the frosting to a piping bag or drizzle with a teaspoon.

TIP: Be careful what peanut butter you use, make sure it doesn't contain Xylitol, which is toxic to dogs

MARSHMALLOW

INGREDIENTS

330g grams superfine sugar (1 1/2 cups)
120 grams cold water (1/2 cup)
20 grams unflavored gelatin (7 teaspoons)
120 grams hot water (1/2 cup)
4 grams vanilla extract (1 teaspoon)
2 tbsp freeze-dried raspberry powder or flavoring
Confectioners' sugar and cornstarch (Equal parts)

METHOD

1. Line a pan with low sides, you could use something like a jellyroll/Swiss roll pan approx. 14x9 (36x23), or 9-inch (22cm) square with parchment paper, letting an excess extend over the sides of the pan,

2. Assemble the Ankarsrum with the plastic beater bowl and balloon whisks
3. Place the sugar and cold water in the plastic beater bowl and beat at speed 3 for 2 minutes.
4. While the sugar is beating, put the hot water in a small bowl and sprinkle gelatine over it, and stir until dissolved.
5. Check the gelatin mixture, if it has started setting, zap it in the microwave for 30 seconds. It must be hot when it is added to the sugar mixture
6. Add gelatin to the sugar mixture, place the white lid on, and mix at full speed for approx. 4-6 minutes. Add flavoring and coloring halfway through. Check after 6 minutes. It should be thick and smooth.
7. Spoon into prepared tray and spread smooth. Place in fridge to set for around 2 hours.

OR

2. Assemble the Ankarsrum with the stainless steel bowl, scraper, and dough roller, with the roller against the edge.
3. Place the sugar and cold water in the stainless steel bowl and beat at speed 3 for 3 minutes.
4. While the sugar is beating, put the hot water in a small bowl and sprinkle gelatine over it, and stir until dissolved. Check the gelatin mixture, if it has started setting, zap in the microwave for 30 seconds. It must be hot when it is added to the sugar mixture
5. Add gelatine to sugar mixture and mix for 8- 10 minutes on high speed. It will eventually come together and be thick and creamy. About halfway through add vanilla and flavouring. It should be thick and smooth.

Mix equal parts of confectioner's sugar and cornstarch and toss marshmallow in to stop it from becoming sticky.

FOCACCIA

INGREDIENTS

7 g instant yeast (2 teaspoons)
360 grams water (1 cup)
12 grams granulated sugar (1 tablespoon)
3 grams kosher salt (1 teaspoon)
14 grams olive oil (1 tablespoon)
500g high-grade bread flour (4 cups)
Olive oil (extra)
Salt (extra)
 Rosemary (optional)

METHOD

1. Spray a 9 x 13 (23x33cm) baking pan) with cooking spray. Line with parchment paper, letting an excess extend over the sides of the pan.
2. Assemble the Ankarsrum with the stainless steel bowl, scraper, and dough roller, with the roller one inch from the edge.
3. Place water, sugar, and yeast in the Ankarsrum stainless steel bowl and leave for 5 minutes.
4. Then add flour, salt, and olive oil and mix for 8 minutes on speed 3.
5. It's important when you are kneading dough that the gluten is fully developed.To test, take a piece of dough slightly smaller than a golf ball and press it flat into a disk on the bench, leave it for a couple of minutes then slowly pull opposite ends of the disk, and if it stretches and you can start to see through it, the gluten is developed. If it rips, place the disk back into the bowl and keep kneading, for a couple more minutes.
6. If ready, cover it with the white lid and place it in a warm spot until doubled.
7. When ready take dough and press into the prepared pan. Poke deep holes randomly in the dough
8. Leave it to rise in a warm spot until nearly doubles again.
9. When the dough is nearly ready to bake preheat the oven to 430°F (220°C)
10. Just before placing in oven drizzle with olive oil and sprinkle with salt and rosemary (if using)
11. Bake for 20 minutes or until golden; if you tap it, it should sound hollow.

Another Option
1. To make breakfast focaccia: Just before baking, instead of sprinkling with salt and rosemary, spread relish to cover the dough and place some bacon on top, then carefully crack 4 – 5 eggs into the holes, Scatter with Mozzarella and parmesan cheese and season with salt and pepper.
2. Cook for 20 minutes or until golden.

PINK BUNS

INGREDIENTS

30 grams bread flour (¼ cup)
120 grams whole milk (½ cup)
180 grams whole milk (¾ cup)
24 grams granulated sugar (2 tablespoons)
7 grams instant yeast (2 teaspoons)
30 grams milk powder (¼ cup)
3 grams kosher salt (1 teaspoon)
1 egg
375 grams bread flour (3 cups)
42 grams butter, room temperature (3 tablespoons)
Egg wash - 1 egg whisked with 1 tablespoon water and
a pinch of salt
200 grams raspberry jam
Icing
240 grams confectioners' sugar (2 cups)
14 grams butter, room temperature (1 tablespoon)
15 grams water (1 tablespoon)
Small drop of pink or red food coloring, to t nt icing pink

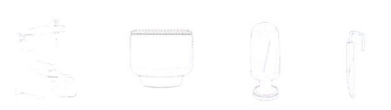

METHOD

1. Assemble the Ankarsrum with the stainless steel bowl, scraper, and dough roller. Place roller 1 inch from edge.
2. Spray a 9 x 13 inch (23x33cm) baking pan with cooking spray. Line with parchment paper, letting an excess extend over the sides of the pan.
3. Place the first portion of milk 120 grams (½ cup) in a microwave bowl and heat until nearly boiling, then add flour and whisk until it thickens into a paste. Transfer to the bowl of your Ankarsrum stainless steel bowl.
4. Add the second portion of milk 180 grams (¾ cup), sugar, yeast, milk powder, salt, egg, and flour to the bowl and beat on speed 3 for 12 minutes. It will be sticky, but you may need to add another one or two tablespoons of flour.
5. Add the butter and mix for a further 3 minutes until incorporated. The dough should be smooth and elastic and pass the windowpane test.
6. Tip the dough out onto a lightly floured surface and bring it into a tight ball. Transfer it to a greased bowl and cover the bowl with plastic wrap. Place the dough in a warm spot and rise until doubled in size, approximately 1 ½ hours.
7. Turn the dough out onto a lightly floured surface.
8. Divide the dough into 12 equal portions, each weighing about 65 grams. Working with one piece of dough at a time, flatten out the piece of dough, then roll it up into a little bal.
9. Repeat with the remaining pieces of dough, keeping the balls slightly apart so they don't touch.
10. Leave the dough balls to rest for 10 minutes, then place them in the prepared pan.
11. Cover the buns with lightly greased plast c wrap and leave to rise again for about an hour.
You want them to puff up and be double in size, and when you press lightly on one, it should leave a small indentation that doesn't quite spring back.
12. When buns are nearly ready to be cooked Preheat oven to 350°F (180°C).
13. Brush buns with egg wash and bake in oven for 15-18 minutes, or until golden brown. Leave to cool in the pan.
14. Place the jam into a piping bag fitted with a round piping tip. Poke a hole in the top of each of the buns using a chopstick. Wiggle it around to make a hole for the jam. Pipe jam into the tops of the buns.
15. Ice with prepared icing.

Icing
Combine confectioners' sugar, butter, and water into a small bowl and mix well. Add coloring, just small amounts at a time. Add more water or sugar to get the correct consistency. It needs to be thick enough to spread, but not too runny.

TORTILLA AND PITA CRISPS

INGREDIENTS

440 grams all-purpose flour (3 ½ cups)
3 grams kosher salt (1 teaspoon)
2.5 grams baking powder (½ teaspoon)
110 grams canola or vegetable oil (½ cup)
120 grams very hot water (½ cup)

METHOD

1. Assemble the Ankarsrum with the stainless steel bowl, scraper, and dough roller, setting the roller approx. ½ inch against the edge.
2. Place flour, salt, and baking powder in the Ankarsrum stainless steel bowl and mix at speed 3 for 1 minute until well combined. Add oil and hot water and keep beating for 3 minutes. The dough should be soft enough to roll easily. If it is a bit dry add more water 1 tablespoon at a time.
3. Take the dough out and roll it into a ball. Spray the bowl lightly and place the dough back into the bowl and cover with the white lid or use another greased bowl and cover it with clingwrap. Allow to stand for 15 minutes.
4. Divide into 8 portions. Roll into balls, then roll out balls very thinly approx. 1/32 inch (1 mm) onto a lightly floured board.
5. Heat a frying pan, spray lightly with cooking oil, and cook tortillas one by one over medium/high heat. When you put the tortilla in the pan, it will almost go slightly translucent It will start making little air pockets, after about 30 seconds, so flip it over for another 30 seconds until it has small golden spots on it. Take it off and leave it to cool on a rack. Tortillas can be reheated in the microwave or wrapped in tin foil and heated in the oven.

PITA CRISPS

Batch of tortillas

METHOD

1. Preheat oven to 430°F (220°C)
2. Take a large sheet pan (don't line it with parchment).
3. Split the pita pockets in half (depending on how thick they are) or just cut them into triangles, approx. 8 triangles per pita, depending on how large you want them.
4. Brush with olive oil and season with kosher salt and dried herbs or bagel seasoning, place a single layer on the tray and bake.
5. Bake for 5 to 10 minutes, checking occasionally to turn over the pita triangles that have gained color, until you have pita chips that are crispy and golden brown to your liking.

PIZZA DOUGH

INGREDIENTS

360 grams water (1 ½ cups)
3 ½ grams instant yeast (1 teaspoon)
625 grams Bread flour (5 cups)
9 grams kosher salt (3 teaspoons)

METHOD

1. Assemble the Ankarsrum with the stainless steel bowl, scraper, and dough roller, and lock the arm in place 1 inch (2-3cm) from the side of the bowl.
2. Place water and yeast in the Ankarsrum stainless steel bowl and leave for 5 minutes.
3. Add flour and salt and beat on speed 3 for 10 minutes until window-pane appears. It's important when you are kneading dough that the gluten is fully developed. To test, take a piece of dough slightly smaller than a golf ball and press it flat into a disk on the bench, leave it for a couple of minutes then slowly pull opposite ends of the disk and if it stretches and if you can start to see through it, the gluten has developed. If it rips, place the disk back into the bowl and keep kneading, for a couple more minutes.
4. Take out of the bowl and roll into a ball, then spray the bowl. Place dough back into the bowl and cover with the white lid, place in a warm place and let rise until it's double in size.
5. Cut into 4 even pieces and roll into balls.
6. Roll out into pizza circles.

Makes 4 medium pizzas

Try this delicious pizza sauce ...

3 tbsp extra virgin olive oil
1 medium onion, very finely chopped
3 cloves garlic, crushed
2 stalks fresh rosemary, leaves finely chopped
1 cup cranberry sauce
1 cup chicken stock
4 tbsp tomato paste
Pinch chili flakes
2 tsp lemon juice

Heat oil in a small saucepan add onion, garlic, and rosemary, and fry over medium heat. Cook for a few minutes until the onion is soft. Add cranberry sauce, stock, tomato paste and chili flakes, and simmer for 10 minutes until slightly thickened. Add lemon juice and season with salt and pepper.

CINNAMON SCROLLS

INGREDIENTS

240 grams whole milk, warm (1 cup)
7 grams instant yeast (2 teaspoons)
76 grams butter, melted (1/3 cup)
50 grams granulated sugar (1/4 cup)
60 grams sour cream (1/4 cup)
1 egg
500 grams all-purpose flour (4 cups)
3 grams kosher salt (1 teaspoon)

Cinnamon mix
165 grams firmly packed brown sugar (3/4 cup)
150 grams butter, room temperature (2/3 cup)
10 grams ground cinnamon (5 teaspoons)
8 grams cornstarch (1 tablespoon)
Icing
112 grams soft cream cheese (1/2 cup)
14 grams soft butter (1 tablespoon)
180 grams confectioners' sugar (1 ½ cups)
15 grams whole milk (1 tablespoon)

METHOD

1. Assemble the Ankarsrum with the stainless steel bowl, scraper, and dough roller, with the roller against the edge.
2. Place half the warm milk and yeast into the Ankarsrum stainless steel bowl and let it stand until foamy, about 10 minutes.
3. Add melted butter, sugar, sour cream, egg, and remaining warm milk into the bowl and mix at low speed for 1 minute.
4. Move the roller to approx. 1 inch from the edge, add flour and salt and turn up to speed 3 for 10 minutes.
The dough should be soft and not too sticky and pass the windowpane test
5. Remove from the bowl and shape dough into a smooth ball.
6. Place the dough ball in a lightly greased bowl, cover loosely, and place in a warm spot until doubled in size.
 Once it has doubled cover in the fridge overnight.
7. Take the dough out of the fridge to slightly warm up and make it easier to roll.
8. Spray a 13x9 inch (33 x 23cm) baking pan with cooking spray and line with parchment paper.
9. In a small bowl, stir together brown sugar, butter, cinnamon, and cornstarch very well. It needs to be very soft, but not melted.
10. Turn out dough onto a lightly floured surface, and roll into a rectangle 18 inches across x12-inches high (46 x 30cm)
11. Spread brown sugar mixture onto dough, stopping ½ inch short of the top.
12. Starting from the dough closest to you roll up into a log, right to the top.
13. Cut into 12 rolls (about 1 ½ inches thick) and tuck the ½ inch part of the dough with no sugar mixture under the roll. Like a little tail.
14.   Place in prepared tin and let it rise until the rolls are puffed up and touching, approx. 30 to 45 minutes. To check if scrolls are ready to bake poke gently with your finger, there should be a small indentation left.
15. While the buns are proving preheat the oven to 350°F (180°C)
16. Bake for about 25 minutes, or until golden. Let cool in the pan for 10 minutes.

Icing
1. Assemble the Ankarsrum with the plastic beater bowl and single wire cookie whisk
2. Place cream cheese and butter in the beater bowl and beat at speed 3 for 4 minutes. Turn to low and
gradually add confectioners' sugar and milk, beating on 2 for a further 4 minutes until fluffy. Spread icing onto scrolls.

PECAN BUNS

INGREDIENTS

240 grams whole milk, warm (1 cup)
7 grams instant yeast (2 teaspoons)
75 grams butter, melted (⅓ cup)
50 grams granulated sugar (¼ cup)
60 grams sour cream (¼ cup)
1 egg
500 grams all-purpose flour (4 cups)
3 grams kosher salt (1 teaspoon)

Cinnamon mix

165 grams firmly packed brown sugar (¾ cup)
150 grams butter, room temperature (2/3 cup)
8 grams ground cinnamon (4 teaspoons)
2 grams ground cardamon (1 teaspoon)
8 grams cornstarch (1 tablespoon)

Pecan topping

150 grams pecan halves (1 ½ cups)
170 grams golden syrup (½ cup)
57 grams butter, room temperature (¼ cup)
110 grams firmly packed brown sugar (½ cup)
4 grams vanilla extract (1 teaspoon)
Pinch of salt

METHOD

1. Assemble the Ankarsrum with the stainless steel bowl, scraper, and dough roller, with the roller against the edge.

2. Place half the warm milk and yeast into the Ankarsrum stainless steel bowl and let stand until foamy, about 10 minutes.

3. Spread pecans over a baking sheet and bake at 350°F (180°C) for 8 to 10 minutes or until golden brown and set aside.

4. Add melted butter, sugar, sour cream, egg and remaining warm milk into the bowl and mix at low speed for 1 minute.

5. Move the roller to approx. 1 inch from the edge and slowly add flour and salt and turn up to speed 3 for 10 minutes.   The dough should be soft and not too sticky and pass the windowpane test

6. Remove from the bowl and shape dough into a smooth ball.

7. Place the dough ball in a lightly greased bowl, cover it loosely, and place it in a warm spot until doubled in size.

8. Once it has doubled, punch it down and roll it out, or cover it in the fridge overnight.

9. Take the dough out of the fridge for about 20-30 minutes to slightly warm up and make it easier to roll.

10. Spray a 13x9-inch (33 x 23cm) baking pan with cooking spray and line it with parchment paper

11. In a microwave-safe container, combine the golden syrup, butter, and brown sugar, and cook for 2 minutes, or until the butter and brown sugar has melted.Add vanilla and salt and mix well.

12. Pour caramel into the baking pan, scatter pecans over the surface, and set aside.

13. In a small bowl, stir together brown sugar, butter, cinnamon, cardamon, and cornstarch very well. The butter needs to be very soft, but not melted.

14. Turn out dough onto a lightly floured surface, and roll it into a rectangle, 18 inches across x 12-inches high (46 x 30cm).

15. Spread the brown sugar mixture onto dough, stopping ½ inch short of the top. Starting from the dough closest to you roll up into a log right to the top.

16. Slice into 12 rolls (about 1 ½ inches thick) and tuck the ½ inch part of the dough with no sugar mixture under the roll. Like a little base. This is so the sugar mixture doesn't leak out while cooking

17 . Place in prepared tin by arranging on top of the caramel and pecans, lightly cover, and let it rise until the rolls are puffed up and touching about   30 to 45 minutes. To check if the scrolls are ready to bake poke gently with your finger, there should be a small indentation left.

18. While the buns are proving, preheat the oven to 350°F (180°C).

19. Bake for about 25 minutes, or until golden. Let it cool in the pan for 10 minutes then tip over to serve.

WHITE TOAST BREAD

INGREDIENTS

625 grams bread flour (5 cups)
420 grams warm water (1 ¾ cups)
10 grams instant yeast (3 teaspoons)
28 grams vegetable oil (2 tablespoons)
15 grams kosher salt (5 teaspoons)
12 grams granulated sugar (1 tablespoon)

METHOD

1. Assemble the Ankarsrum with the stainless steel bowl, dough knife, and dough roller, an inch from the edge.
2. Place all ingredients in the Ankarsrum stainless steel bowl and mix on speed 3 for 10 minutes, until the dough is soft, and at the windowpane stage (see below).
3. Divide the dough into 4 even pieces and roll into balls, cover, and set aside for 15 minutes.
4. Prepare two 9 x 5 inch loaf tins (22cm x 12cm) spray well with cooking spray and line with parchment paper, extending paper over the sides.
5. Lightly roll each piece of dough into tight balls, and place 2 balls of dough into each tin. Cover with a tea towel and leave in a warm place until doubled in size.
6. Preheat oven to 390°F (200°C).
7. Bake for 30 minutes or until the crust is golden brown. Remove from tins onto a wire rack and leave to cool for at least 10 minutes before slicing.

TIP: It's important when you are kneading dough that the gluten is fully developed. To test, take a piece of dough slightly smaller than a golf ball and press it flat into a disk on the bench, leave it for a couple of minutes then slowly pull opposite ends of the disk, and if it stretches and you can start to see through it, the gluten has developed. If it rips, place the disk back into the bowl and keep kneading, for a couple more minutes.

www.ingramcontent.com/pod-product-compliance
Lightning Source LLC
Chambersburg PA
CBRC090825120626
46547CB00008B/614